"The Model"   William Mortensen

The Model

A Book on the Problems of Posing

by

WILLIAM MORTENSEN

CAMERA CRAFT PUBLISHING COMPANY

376 Sutter Street   San Francisco, 8 Calif.

Other Books by

WILLIAM MORTENSEN

New Projection Control

Flash in Modern Photography

Outdoor Portraiture

Monsters & Madonnas

The Command To Look

Print Finishing

Pictorial Lighting

First Edition

First Printing March 1937

Second Printing November 1937

Third Printing September 1940

Fourth Printing September 1943

Fifth Printing December 1944

Sixth Printing July 1946

Printed in the United States of America
by THE MERCURY PRESS, San Francisco

To Myrdith

TABLE OF CONTENTS

7

FOREWORD

The aim of this book is to give the student of photography some basis for self-criticism in his posing and arranging of the model. The basis of this criticism is necessarily largely negative—as all worthwhile and useful criticism of creative work is bound to be. It is only weaklings and incompetents who plead for "constructive criticism". The constructive, positive part of any art-work must be furnished by the artist-pupil himself. The instructor or critic cannot "constructively" criticize a student's picture or story or symphony without, in effect, doing the work that the student should do. It is true that a presentable picture (or story, or symphony) may be thus produced; but it will be, fundamentally, the teacher's accomplishment.

Therefore, warnings and negative precepts compose a great deal of this book. To give positive and concrete instruction on *just how* to pose a model is as impossible as to give instruction on just how to write a song. But there are, in both cases, certain errors and traps that the incautious or inexperienced worker is liable to, and which he may be warned away from.

Some of the faults that are hereafter represented may seem, because of their isolation, ridiculously obvious, and nothing that any reasonable person would perpetrate. However, specimens of nearly every one of the typical errors that are isolated and described in this book may be found in the pages of photographic journals and annuals, in volumes devoted to the exploitation of nude photography, and on the august walls of international salons.

Study of the graphic and plastic arts of the past provides the only proper basis for the pictorial arrangement of the human figure.

Although art in the past has revealed many strange revolutions of taste, there may be traced, even through the most aberrated periods, a constant tradition of good design. Application of this tradition to the problem of posing a model before the camera will lead one, not to a series of stock poses, but to the principles that underlie good posing.

There is definite need for a book that approaches the plastic problems of the human body from the photographic angle. My conviction on this point has lately been strengthened by certain albums that pretended to offer advice and inspiration on these problems. These luxurious volumes are, in my opinion, thoroughly hypocritical in their pious avowals. Such instruction and inspiration as they may offer lie, not in the realm of art, but in the field of biology. Vulgar in conception, crude in lighting, execrable in photography, they seem to be aimed no higher than the parlour tables of sporting houses. Indeed, better taste and better photography are to be found in some of the *sub rosa* publications that are denied the use of the mails.

For the basic plan and method of this book I owe a large debt to George Bridgman, in whose anatomy class many years ago at the Art Students' League I first came to appreciate the dignity and logic of the human body. I am also indebted to J. C. Flügl's *Psychology of Clothes* and to Laurene Hempstead's *Color and Line in Dress* for valuable material in Chapters Two and Seven of Part One.

WILLIAM MORTENSEN

Laguna Beach, California
November, 1936

The Model

A Book on the Problems of Posing

INTRODUCTION

Giotto's Goat.

About the year 1286, according to tradition, the painter Cimabue, riding over the hills near Vespignano, came upon a shepherd boy who, while watching his flock, had sketched a goat on a piece of slate. Amazed at the life-like quality of the sketch, so the story goes, Cimabue took the boy, Ambrogiotto Bondone, back to Florence with him as his pupil. The later accomplishment of this boy, better known simply by his nickname of Giotto, marked a turning point in the development of art in Europe.

Giotto's goat is, so far as I know, one of the earliest mentioned living models in western art. The boy's naive return to natural sources was a gesture significant in the history of Italian art, which was just then struggling against the lifeless formalism of Byzantium.

The model is a crucial factor in the graphic arts, a factor the importance of which we are apt to forget. Without the model as a living, breathing, reacting *fact*, graphic art is prone to fall into rigid formalism on the one hand, and into undisciplined improvisation on the other. Through the meeting of artist and model the miracle of the incalculable, the impulse of the accidental, is brought to pass and incorporated into the work of art. Giotto's goat is the first of a noble line that have made their scantly appreciated contribution to the world's pictorial wealth. In going through a great art gallery, such as the Louvre, the Metropolitan, or the Pitti Palace, how seldom we give any thought to the nameless army of people "behind

14

the pictures", those numberless men and women, unremembered save as artists have recorded them in paint, whose warm and living presence was the stimulus that brought forth works of art.

The identity of a very few of these models is known to the public. Nearly everyone who has seen the Mona Lisa knows the story of La Gioconda and the several years that she sat for Leonardo while he struggled to capture the essence of this enigmatic personality. Well known also is the romance of Goya and the Duchess of Alba, the uncouth painter and the lady of quality, and the inspiration that Romney derived from "frail Emma", and the many, many pictures that he painted of her. We read also that the quality of Rossetti's work was inextricably bound up in the personality of his model, Elizabeth Siddal, who later became his wife. The fact that the contribution of these ladies, and of others who have played similar roles in art history, was not solely aesthetic and disinterested, does not confuse the issue. The sex impulse and the art impulse are fundamentally very closely related. Both are profound, irresistible, and immeasurably subtle.

More than any other of the graphic arts, photography is dependent on the presence of the model. For instance, it is not possible in the model's absence, as in the other arts, to work up the finished picture from the preliminary sketches. Nor is it feasible photographically, though just barely possible, to make a composite of Mary's face, Susie's body, and Anabelle's hands. In other words, the model must be *there*, and she must closely conform in all points to that which she is to represent. And when she is there in front of the camera, and she proves to conform physically to that which is desired, the problem of the model is but partly solved; for she must be made to understand and be brought to express that which the photographer is seeking to tell in his picture.

Corpus Delicti.

Generally the inexperienced photographer is embarrassed and surprised on discovering how unmanageable an apparently complaisant model can be. Like someone who has incautiously committed a murder, he is left with an awkward *corpus delicti* on his hands, a certain amount of flesh which he must dispose of gracefully, but which, in his mounting panic, becomes increasingly unmanageable with his every desperate effort to do something with it.

Perhaps he has heard that *natural* poses are the best. So he may attempt a *laissez-faire* attitude and let nature take its course in the matter of posing. But he soon learns that, photographically at least, Nature is an unpleasing, stupid, lumpy, blowsy wench. The artist in any medium is unhappily compelled to cope with the damnable perversity of things, but none so much as the photographer is aware of the utter non-cooperativeness and the implacable stubbornness of Nature. The painter may adjust perspectives and warp arms and legs into attitudes that are more becoming or compatible to his design. But the photographer must take things as they are. The arms and legs that he deals with are flesh and bone, and are uncompromisingly unmalleable.

The photographer with a model is a Creator with a little bit of Chaos. He must learn the Word that will give it form.

Two Types of Adjustment.

There are two channels through which the photographer works in securing a desired pictorial result from a model, viz.:

1. Physical.
2. Psychological.

He must first secure the desired physical conformation with his pictorial intent. To do this requires a background of acquaintance with the forms and traditions in plastic and graphic arrangements. He must further have a sharp eye for a considerable number of more or less standardized plastic faults that the unguided human body almost inevitably falls into, and he must know how to correct these faults.

In addition to these physical adjustments, the artist must establish mental contact with his model. He must lift the dead weight of the model by his enthusiasm. He must give of his mental energy to plant the thought in the physical form. He must draw forth the expressive abilities of the model and must aid the model in shaping this expression to the strict physical limitations of the pictorial medium.

The majority of the bad results that photographers obtain in dealing with models are due to their attempt to work from a purely psychological basis. Evidently photographers believe that if the model has a lofty emotion and thinks great thoughts, great pictures are inevitable. Ten million bad pictures bear witness to the falsity of this belief. Pictorially speaking, great thoughts and acute physical anguish are practically impossible to distinguish, and oftentimes a caption is required to inform us whether the model is suffering from melancholia or the megrims.

Such grotesque posturing and grimacing (full of significance to the model, but meaningless to the beholder) can be eliminated only by creating the pose on a physical and objective basis. Bodily expression in pictures bears a close relation to the objective and plastic language of *pantomime*. Pantomime is not in the least concerned with what the actor thinks, but is very much concerned with what the *beholder* thinks that the actor thinks. Similarly, the actual feelings and thoughts of the model in a picture matter not at all; what does matter is whether the beholder is given an *impression* of thought and feeling.

In exacting from the model this physical obedience and mental cooperation, the artist becomes a showman. In common with all showmen, his ego must dominate. There is much self flattery in posing a picture. The model is the means through which the artist realizes *himself*. The "Greatest Show on Earth" was not Barnum's collection of freaks, but Mr. Barnum himself. Florenz Ziegfeld traditionally "glorified the American Girl", but even more did he glorify Ziegfeld. In a sense, art is merely a by-product of the artist's quest for self-gratification.

These two channels — physical and psychological — through which the artist deals with his model, are fundamental and important, and form the basis of the division of material in this book. The first part deals with objective physical adjustments, the second and

17

third parts with psychological problems of expression and procedure.

Three Kinds of Models.

The photographer will find, in his association with models, that there are three different conditions of working. It is necessary to understand and discriminate between these three conditions, as each is fitted to a distinct type of model and each results in a different type of picture. These are the three conditions:

1. The artist is dominant.
2. The model is dominant.
3. There is cooperation between the two.

Although an experienced and accomplished model may be able to adapt himself or herself to any of these three conditions of working, the three conditions demand three different types of model, with widely different equipment and qualifications. These three types we may for brevity's sake designate as follows:

1. The passive type.
2. The personal type.
3. The cooperative type.

In order to get the best work out of models, it is necessary to appreciate the qualities of the three different types, to be able to choose them according to type, and to understand the different sort of treatment that each type requires. Discussion of these matters will be found in Part Three.

"The World Without Clothes".

But with physical adjustments and with psychological problems with passive, personal or cooperative models, the basis of it all remains the physical human *body*. The plastic element is the basic pictorial element. If the plastic element is missing, or is wrongly handled, the picture will be a poor thing, no matter how carefully thought out or how truly felt it may be. The medium of expression is the body, and it is of the utmost importance to learn to deal with this very concrete problem.

Many photographers never have occasion to deal with unclothed models. But under all clothes lies the nude human body. Clothes are conditioned and determined by the body that wears them. The posing of the clothed body may be fully understood only in terms of the conformation of the nude body. Therefore, emphasis will be given in the following pages to the posing of the nude, with considerable attention to the anatomical approach. Even though he does not intend to specialize in this field, a certain amount of experience in photographing the nude is most advantageous to anyone going into pictorial work. The portraitist also can profit by such experience: he can no doubt more becomingly arrange Mrs. Mountford-Jones if his mind can clearly picture just how Mrs. Mountford-Jones is constituted underneath her expensive gown.

Such familiarity with the body breeds, not contempt, but rather a wholesome acceptance of the normal. Instead of an object of prurient curiosity, the nude body becomes, by familiarity, merely the plastic basis of pictorial art.

That Which is in Front of the Camera.

Photographers have for a long time been gazing with hypnotic absorption at this mechanical-optical marvel, the camera. Let them lift their eyes and consider that which is in front of the camera. There waits the model—Mona Lisa in the person of Mary Jones. What are they going to do with her? It would be well if photographers could forget for a while the expensive camera and its marvelous insides and the impressive array of chemicals in the closet under the stairs, and concentrate solely and definitely on the model. For it is through the model—whether it be a goat or a duchess—that life is made to stir in the dead substance of the picture.

PART ONE

The Physical Basis

CHAPTER ONE

The Problem

The first section of this book will deal with the physical aspects of the problem of posing a model before the camera. Many questions arise in posing that are of a purely mechanical nature. These are best understood and most readily solved if they are studied from an entirely objective, impersonal angle.

We are by habit so prone to assume and admit into consideration the personality and emotional qualities of the model that it is rather difficult to acquire the requisite objective and disinterested attitude. Personality and emotion are important matters in pictorial representation; but at this point they are irrelevant and misleading. Personality and emotion can realize themselves only on an adequate *plastic basis*. Until the body can be made to furnish this proper plastic basis, it is futile to try to progress beyond it.

The Mechanical Approach.

The peculiar object pictured in Fig. 1 is what artists call a "lay figure". It is a fully articulated and adjustable wooden manikin. In the absence of a living model, artists use such a figure to check and study poses.

For the purposes of the first part of this book, our model, Mary

Figure 1

Jones, will be regarded merely as a lay figure. A more delicately articulated lay figure, no doubt, but needing just as much mechanical adjustment. Until the proper adjustments are made, Mary is just as disorganized physically as the manikin here illustrated. We are not for a moment concerned with what Mary thinks or feels, but merely with the mechanical adjustment and plastic relationships of her articulated members. The fundamental faults that occur in posing have nothing to do with expression: they are simply bad design.

Negative Precepts.

The study of the plastic relationships of the body will be treated principally in negative terms—in terms of errors to avoid. The reason for this approach is easily understood and justified.

The fluidity of the human body is infinite. With the same model on two successive days it is utterly impossible to duplicate a pose. Hard-and-fast positive suggestions would definitely limit one's appreciation of the plastic potentialities of the human body.

Faults in posing, however, are concrete. They are readily pointed out, and are easily identified and classified. They are the logical angle of approach to the problem. The standard which is assumed in pointing out these errors is that of traditional usage and generally accepted ideas of grace and harmony in the older graphic arts.

As will appear in the following pages, these faults are fairly numerous. Obviously, there are practical difficulties involved in avoiding all errors—or traces of them, at least—under the actual conditions of working. Avoidance of one error may lead into another. There is also the possibility, which will be later discussed, that certain errors may be intentionally introduced for the sake of greater emphasis or emotional effect.

It should be understood in advance that the errors which we are about to consider, although all unpleasant, are not of equal seriousness.

There are, roughly speaking, two grades of errors. There are *primary errors* that violate basic plastic laws. These must be avoided under all circumstances. There are also *secondary errors* which produce unpleasant disturbances in the picture. So far as possible, these should be avoided likewise, but their occurrence is sometimes inevitable. If they do not occur too conspicuously or too numerously, they may be tolerated.

We will consider in turn the plastic qualities of each part of the body, and note the errors that are likely to arise in posing it. In Chapter Six we will classify these errors along the lines indicated above.

Correcting Errors.

In photographic practice there are three different stages at which errors in posing may be detected and dealt with by correction or elimination.

1. At the time of the sitting.
2. In checking over the proofs.
3. In subjecting the negative to Projection Control or other control methods.

1. It is at the time of the sitting, of course, that the largest amount of work takes place, both in the positive creation of a plastic composition and in the negative elimination of errors.

2. Errors that are overlooked at the time of shooting often appear with shocking obviousness in the proofs. If the error is serious and conspicuous, particularly if it belongs to the first class of errors mentioned above, the proof should be dropped in the waste basket without further ado.

3. Occasionally an error that appears in the proof may be corrected in the final print by the use of control methods. Such an error as a "trap"*, for example, may yield to Projection Control. With the use of the Bromoil Transfer method more extensive correction is possible, and even a certain amount of structural alteration.

Lighting and Structure.

Reference will be made to lighting problems. While, strictly speaking, lighting and posing belong to different categories, yet there is sufficient relationship to warrant treating them together. Certain of the errors hereafter mentioned are primarily errors in lighting.

Bad lighting and bad posing are similar in that they both violate the essential plastic structure of the subject. Lighting, no matter how beautiful or spectacular, cannot salvage a bad pose; but a good pose and structure may be irreparably damaged by bad lighting.

The type of illumination that I have designated as the "Basic Light"** will be taken as the standard. It is primarily a structural light. Additional suggestions will be made for the use of the "Dynamic" and "Plastic" Lights.

*Chapter Three, seq.

**Pictorial Lighting by William Mortensen. Camera Craft, 1935.

CHAPTER TWO

The Head and Face.

The human body is a structure—a relationship of parts. The best posing of the body is that which best and most clearly expresses this structure, the relationship of the parts, and their articulations.

The head is not an egg, though careless draughtsmen sometimes represent it as such. Rather, the head is a somewhat domed cubical mass, supported by the muscular column of the neck. The best photographic representation of the head will show, without harshness, the well-defined planes that bound the head, and the transitions between them. (Figure 2.) Bad representation of the head is that which, by bad choice of angle, distorts or falsifies this structure, or which, by retouching or soft focus, reduces it to a mask in putty or an unstructured blob of cotton wool.

The pictorialist is interested in the head as a structural element of the whole figure. Hence, he regards it and represents it from many aspects and angles. The portraitist, however, is interested almost exclusively in the front plane of the head, the facade, the so-called human face. This plane resolves itself into a series of structurally related sub-planes. As with the whole head, the best rendering of the face is that which gives the firmest and most concise expression of its structure. Bad portraiture always in some manner violates the structure of the face.

Angles of Presentation.

The head rotates to right or left through an angle of about a

Figure 2

Figure 2

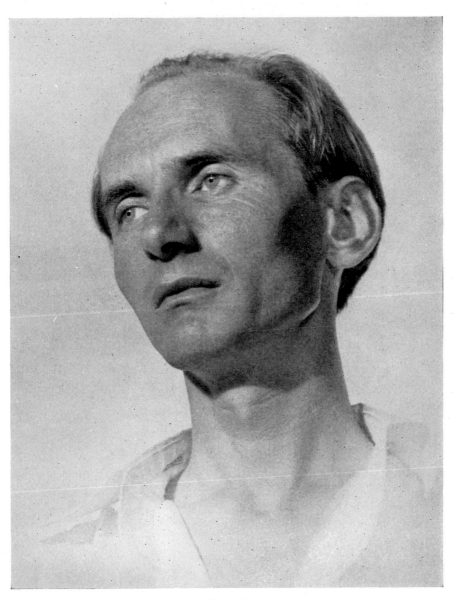

Figure 3

hundred and twenty degrees. It may also be tipped to right or left, or to front or back. This large range of adjustment, together with a considerable choice of camera angles, provides the artist with an almost infinite variety of aspects for presenting the head.

For conventional portraiture the useful angles range from full-face to profile, with a number of intermediate three-quarter views. For pictorial work, the range may be extended past the profile angle to a three-quarter rear view.

The primary requisite for the profile angle is, of course, that the model have an interesting profile. Unless the aim of the picture is flattery, it is not necessary that the profile be a beautiful one, for a startling or fantastic contour may be made the very *point d'appui* of the picture. Since the choice of the profile angle is made, presumably, to display the profile, the subject should be lighted with this in mind. Basic, Contour, or Semi-Silhouette light is best in this case. Seldom is the Dynamic or Plastic Light justified with a profile.

The use of the full-face angle depends likewise on the pictorial aim of the artist. For more or less flattering conventional portraiture, this angle is not adapted to faces of noticeable asymmetry, faces that are unduly round, or to faces in which the eyes are too closely placed. But if these aberrations are to be emphasized for pictorial purposes, the full-face angle may well prove the most effective.

The profile and the full-face are both somewhat abstract and conventionalized versions of the face: one presents the face in terms of a contour, the other in terms of a map. They suggest, therefore, the use of the conventionalized illumination of the Basic Light. A three-quarter view is both more familiar and gives a completer impression of the structure of the head. The fullest possible rendering of the structural masses and planes of the head is given by a three-quarter angle from a viewpoint slightly below the center of the face. This angle gives a clear impression of all three of the principal planes of the head. (Figure 3.)

Since it is less stylized than either profile or full-face, and also since it presents a bolder separation of the structural elements of the

Figure 4   Figure 5

face, the three-quarter view more frequently demands the use of the Plastic or Dynamic Light.

A fault that is apt to occur in using the three-quarter angle of the head is the *split profile*. A split profile results when the tip of the nose comes just even with the line of the cheek, projects just beyond it, or falls barely short of it. (Figure 4.) This effect is unpleasantly equivocal: the line of the cheek should be either definitely stayed away from (Figure 5), or else definitely broken. The eye further from the camera may also become involved in a split profile. The angle of the head should be so adjusted that this eye is either definitely included or unmistakably excluded. Avoid having mere eyelashes or a slight fragment of the eye project beyond the bridge of the nose. (Figure 4.) With the three-quarter view mentioned above, in which the nose definitely breaks the line of the cheek, it is generally necessary, in order to include a proper amount of the eye, either to raise the camera slightly or to tip the head slightly toward

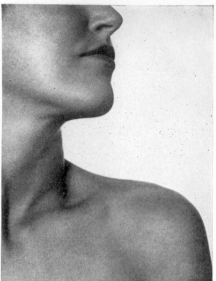

Figure 6 *Figure 7*

the camera. (Figure 6.) An analogous fault occurs when the extreme tip of the ear projects past the temple. Such an excrescence may sometimes be removed from the print; but it is better to arrange the head so that the ear either appears unashamedly as an ear or does not appear at all.

Examples of the split profile appear not infrequently in the work of Holbein and other master painters. Thus there might appear to be august precedent for the use of this angle. Painters, however, are able to adjust the perspective and foreshortening, thereby minimizing the disagreeable effect. In photography the split profile is almost always unpleasing.

Another error that not infrequently occurs in profiles is one that we may call the *cul-de-sac*. This results when the chin is strongly turned toward the shoulder, which is presented flat to the camera, and the background is strongly illuminated. (The *cul-de-sac* is most likely to appear with Semi-Silhouette lighting, with which it is most conspicuous; but it may also occur with the Basic Light.) Under

Figure 8   Figure 9

these circumstances, there is, between chin and shoulder, an unpleasantly conspicuous light area. (Figure 7.) This area appears
all the whiter for being nearly enclosed by the darker masses of
shoulder and chin. When one looks at the picture, the attention is
immediately sucked into the *cul-de-sac*, whence it has difficulty in
extricating itself. This fault is closely allied to the "trap", which
will be discussed in the next chapter.

When a *cul-de-sac* appears in a proof, it may in most cases be
eliminated in making the final print. The elimination is accomplished by Projection Control—darkening the objectionable area
by careful "local printing".

In passivity, the head tends to remain balanced upright on its
pivot. *Tipping the head* to right or left, or to front or back, suggests
movement and action. A full-face view is most frequently formal in
its implication. When the face is in repose and the shoulders are
level, the head *must not be tipped*. In Figure 8, the angle of the head
is clearly at variance with the thought of the picture. Under such

Figure 12   Figure 13

circumstances even a slight variation from the vertical is unpleasant.

In such a portrait as Figure 9, for instance, it is advisable in projecting the negative* to make certain that the vertical axis of the face is parallel to the side of the picture. However, when thought, action, or animation is implied, it is generally demanded that the head be tipped. Note that the head is tipped in Figure 10 *(Windblown)*, although the angle is full-face. The animation of the expression, the swing of the hair, all require that the head be tipped. If this picture is framed with the features vertical, it immediately becomes stiff and uncomfortable, and at the same time loses a certain feminine delicacy.

When the head is tipped, it is always necessary to compensate for this action by raising the shoulder on the side toward which the head is tipped. *Windblown* and Figure 11 demonstrate this compensating action of the shoulders. Raising the shoulder on the side opposite to that toward which the head is tipped—as is not infrequently done

---

* "Framing" the negative during projection allows some scope for adjusting the inclination of the head. Adjustment at this time is, of course, subject to the same principles that govern the posing of the model.

"*Windblown*" William Mortensen

Figure 10

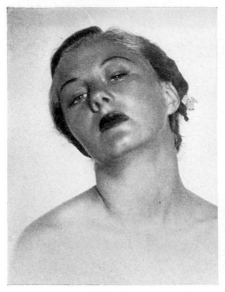

Figure 14   Figure 15

by ill-advised photographers—simply increases the impression of unbalance. (Figure 12.) The model seems to lunge into the picture, and to be in immediate danger of falling out of it.

Models striving misguidedly for coyness are apt to tuck in the chin and tip the head toward the camera. Others, seeking to express blasé hauteur, thrust out the chin and tip back the head. The former effort results in exaggeration of the brow, the latter in exaggeration of the jaw. (Figure 13 and Figure 14.) Bad foreshortening occurs in either case, and both effects, except with definite pictorial intent, are best avoided.

Bowing the head, in three-quarter or profile views, almost always creates, especially if the eyes are downcast, an unpleasantly negative effect. Only with one thought—that of modesty—is this pose justified. Even when the thought of the picture is that of deepest grief and dejection, it is best realized pictorially with the head held erect. (E.g., Guido's *Ecce Homo.*)

It is a favorite trick of inexperienced models to tilt the head

Figure 11

sharply backward. This posture lends them, they imagine, glamour and fascination. (Elderly women resort to it for still another reason that I will mention presently.) With full-face, or nearly full-face angles, this pose is disagreeable, as we have just seen, because of its exaggeration of the jaw. With three-quarter or profile views, this pose should be used with discretion, as it may very readily become strained or melodramatic. (Figure 15.)

Details of Individual Features.

In general, the eyes should appear to look in about the same direction as the head is turned. (Figure 5.) In three-quarter and profile angles, the eyes are apt, when they are actually looking in the same direction as the face, to seem to be turned further from the camera than the face is. In order to correct this impression it is frequently necessary for the model to "cheat" by turning the eyes slightly toward the camera. Eyes so turned that they show a large glint of white suggest one of the subversive emotions—suspicion, jealousy, flirtation, or fear, and they should not be so displayed unless some such thought is meant to be conveyed. (Figure 16.) In portraits it is usually essential that the eyes be shown; but in pictures with the emphasis on the plastic qualities, particularly in nudes, an advantageous impression of impersonality is gained by downcast eyes.*

Eyes that are abnormally prominent should not be represented looking directly at the camera, unless the intent is to give them pictorial emphasis—humorous, in the Eddie Cantor manner, or tragic, in the Peter Lorre manner. Eyes of this sort are least conspicuous in a three-quarter view with the lids lowered. They may be further mitigated by raising the front lighting unit** a foot or eighteen inches. By this expedient the brows are more heavily shadowed, and the apparent depth of the orbit is increased.

A different problem is presented by narrow "squint" eyes. The problem is in a considerable degree psychological, for people with

---

*E.g., Youth or Nude Study in Monsters and Madonnas. Camera Craft. 1936.

**Pictorial Lighting, pg. 31.

Figure 16

this sort of eyes are, as a rule, shy and retiring, and the narrowing of the eyes is a defensive action which the strange surroundings of the photographer's studio are especially apt to call forth. Therefore, it is necessary to reassure such a model and place the sitting on as unimposing and friendly a basis as possible. Eyes with this tendency are shown to most flattering advantage in a full-face view. The head should be slightly depressed, the chin down, and the eyes directed to a point slightly above the *camera*. The best illumination is provided by a Basic Light somewhat modified by pulling the front unit twelve or eighteen inches to one side, so that the light does not shine directly in the subject's eyes.

Tilting the head back too sharply, in a full-face or three-quarter view, presents a very disagreeable aspect of the nose. The nostrils appear cavernous and become the most conspicuous element in the picture. (Figure 14.) This pose is, unhappily, characteristic of a certain type of "art photography". The model is registering something tremendous in the way of emotion, the exact variety of which lies beyond the experience of the present writer.

It is perhaps superfluous to add that noses that are strangely shaped should *not* be presented in profile, unless this malformation is the actual point of the picture. Such proboscidiferous characters as Cyrano de Bergerac, for example, demand profile, or near profile, for their fullest realization.

Large and spreading ears are a characteristic and amusing detail in many small children. However, doting mothers frequently envisage their offspring's ears as small and shell-like; so it generally behooves the photographer to take precautions to avoid emphasizing these features. Protruding ears are, of course, most apparent in a straight-on full-face view, particularly if too low a camera angle is chosen, or the sitter's head is tipped back. If it is desired to retain the full-face angle, the emphasis on the ears may be considerably reduced by raising the camera. Turning the head, even slightly, to the side will also much diminish this emphasis, and in a three-quarter view the ears, though perhaps not shell-like, will not be conspicuous.

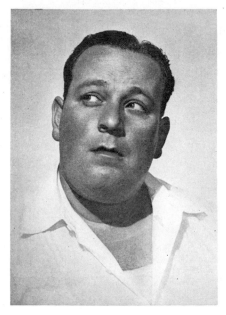 

Figure 17   Figure 18

Elderly women with several chins and hanging jowls are a particularly trying problem for the photographer. Most of them have discovered, by careful study of themselves in the mirror, that, by carrying the chin high, it is possible to diminish somewhat the multiplicity of chins and to erase part of the heavier lines of the neck. So, when they sit for their picture, they immediately resort to this (as they suppose) beautifying expedient. They accomplish, however, the exact opposite of what they desire. The thrust-out chin appears heavier and grosser than it really is, and all wrinkles in the neck, all over-hanging jowls, are revealed unmercifully. This posture also exaggerates the nostrils in a very ugly and equine fashion as described above.

Instead, a sitter that presents such a problem should be advised to hold the head naturally erect, with the chin neither tucked in nor aggressively out-thrust. Raise the camera a foot or eighteen inches above the level of the face. Then instruct the subject to lean forward slightly at the waist, and at the same time to raise the face. In a picture taken from this angle the heaviness of the lower part of the face is much reduced. By leaning forward, the subject's body is made to appear less bulky. For a flattering account of heavy or portly people, the procedure above described is the best solution. Figure 17 shows the subject "as is", with the camera level with the face. Figure 18 was taken with the camera raised and the subject leaning forward slightly.

The same procedure may be adapted to compensating for weakness or excess of chin. If the chin recedes, the camera should be lowered, with the subject's head held erect or tipped slightly away from the camera. For a jutting chin and a harsh jaw an opposite procedure is followed: the camera is raised and the head is held erect or tipped forward slightly.

A face with a short upper lip never appears to good advantage smiling. The unfortunate effect is further emphasized by the chin being tucked in. Such a face is better presented unsmiling, in a three-quarter view, and with the chin well up. An upper lip of fairly generous length is required for a smile of good pictorial quality.

"There Are Smiles—"

The smile is so momentary and fleeting a manifestation that the greatest of care must be exercised in perpetuating it. The majority of pictured smiles convey the same impression of grotesque and uneasy strain that we find in snapshots of people walking—with one foot eternally poised in mid-air. A pictured smile that is pleasing and that is permanent in its charm is very rare indeed. Yet, photographically speaking, we are every day hemmed in, besieged and bombarded by smiles. Acres of gleaming white ivory challenge us from billboards, newspapers, motion picture screens, and commercial portraits, and even pursue us into chaster pictorial precincts.

We may assign photographic smiles to four different classes, only one of which is pictorially tolerable.

Figure 19

First, there is what is known as the *zizzy smile*. I include no illustration of the pure type of the zizzy smile, but thousands of examples may be found in screen magazines and tooth-paste advertisements. It is joyless and violent—a veritable explosion of incisors and bicuspids.

Then there is the *grudging smile*. This also is too familiar to require demonstrating. It results when the photographer insists on a smile and the bedevilled subject finally yields to the extent of lifting an upper lip in a perfunctory grimace that does not conceal the resentment smouldering in the eyes.

Third, there is the *solar-plexus smile*. Or, by analogy with that fine phrase "belly laugh", it might be called the "belly smile". This, unlike those described above, is a natural and spontaneous expression, a sudden overflowing of animal joy. (Figure 19.) With an ebullient model a smile of this sort is very readily obtained. Unfortunately, although it is actually spontaneous and sincere, the excess and suddenness of this smile cause it to have a violent "zizzy" quality. The sense of restraint and control, so necessary to pictorial representation, is missing.

39

Finally, there is the *controlled smile*. The physical manifestation is here kept within bounds. (Figure 20.) Whether or not an actual joyous emotion is present is of no account. What is important is that the expression *appears* to be spontaneous, *appears* to be joyous, and does not rend the picture asunder with the violence of its presentation.

The smile is a pictorial element that should be used very sparingly. Attractive at first, it palls rapidly. The monotonous fixity of expression in time arouses at first passive annoyance, then active resentment. It is significant that smiles appear but rarely on the faces pictured by the great masters of the past. Franz Hals represented smiles more frequently than most artists, but he was always careful to hold them within pictorial bounds. The famous smile of Leonardo's Mona Lisa is painted with such great restraint that some persons have disputed its very existence.

Combination of Faults.

Up to this point we have regarded the various facial flaws and aberrations as occurring separately. Unfortunately for the human race, the flaws sometimes appear in groups. This greatly complicates the problem of compensation. "Just what", enquires the harassed amateur, "does one do with a subject whose receding chin demands that the head be tipped away from the camera, whose large jowls demand that the head be tipped toward the camera, whose protruding ears make a front view out of the question, and whose fantastic nose makes a profile unthinkable?" This question touches closely upon a principal cause of the heavy mortality rate of photographers.

To seek to find by sheer cerebration the exact position, camera angle, and lighting that would compensate for such a combination would doubtless prove futile. In cases in which the photographer is confronted with one of Nature's quainter jokes, the wisest and (in the long run) most economical procedure is for him to take a large number of exposures, not less than six dozen. Let these exposures cover all reasonably possible changes in arrangement, camera angle, costume and lighting. Under these circumstances the photog-

Figure 20

rapher may reasonably hope that Chance, which has so strangely scrambled the features of his subject, will, for a change, work to his advantage and bring forth one or two poses that are acceptable.

Sensitive Points.

Most sitters will prove to be uncomfortably conscious of some one flaw, will go to great pains to cover it up, and will protest strenuously if it appears in the proofs. The photographer will find that there is much difference between his men and his women sitters in the type of flaw that they are sensitive about. Women, as a rule, are most conscious of flaws in the *general effect*, of faults in structure. Conversely, they may be aggressively proud of what they regard as their good structural points — a fine profile, or well - modelled shoulders. Men, on the other hand, are seldom conscious of general faults in structure. But they are apt to be very sensitive about details, such as small marks of age or dissipation.

Among women, the most sensitive point, and the thing they most dread to show in their pictures, is obesity. This fear drives them into extreme and foolish measures for its correction, as I have already mentioned. Among men, the touchy point is *loss of hair*.

Scanty hair may be somewhat concealed by a judicious use of "local printing" with an aperture board*. By means of shadowing along the edge of the hair, the hair-line may be perceptibly lowered.

Arrangement of the Hair.

The arrangement of the hair belongs definitely among the problems of physical adjustment. Many pictures, otherwise acceptable, are spoiled by oversights in dealing with the hair.

The arrangement of the hair must conform to and develop the anatomical structure of the head. Any arrangement that contradicts or violates the essentially domed contour of the skull is, therefore, bad. Among the confections of hairdressers the most frequent fault arises from failure to realize that, as the face is symmetrical, the

---

*New Projection Control. Chapter Five. Camera Craft. 1942.

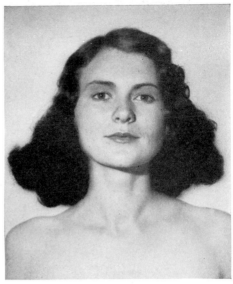

Figure 21   *Figure 22*

hair above it should also partake of this balance. Despite the momentary dictates of fashion, a woman's hair should never be arranged (for photographic purposes) so that it is unequal in mass on the two sides of the head. Compare Figure 21 and 28. (The implication of movement or action, of course, allows for unbalanced arrangement—cf. *Windblown*, Figure 10.) Photographers are frequently obliged to use a three-quarter angle on a subject that would otherwise appear to best advantage in full face, because only in the three-quarter angle is it possible to conceal the disturbing unbalance of the hair.

If the subject's hair is black, or nearly so, care should be taken in arranging it so that it does not appear in large masses. If it does, it will usurp too much of the black area of the picture. Black elements in a picture should be regarded as a condiment—essential and stimulating when sparingly used, deleterious and disastrous when used in excess.

The size of the coiffure should not overbalance the apparent strength of the neck. (Figure 22.) This danger is especially present

Figure 23   Figure 24

with dark hair. Pictorially, blond hair is less heavy.

A contrary danger should also be mentioned. Large women are apt mistakenly to affect a tight headdress. Instead of reducing the size of their faces, as they fondly hope, this device has a precisely opposite effect. The tightness and compactness of the coiffure emphasizes the bulk of the face—and the photographic result is something like Humpty Dumpty in a toupe. (Figure 23.) Generally speaking, a large woman will secure a more flattering picture by loosening her hair and softening its contours. (Figure 24.)

The apparent shape and proportions of the face are susceptible to much alteration by various changes in hairdress. Wrong choice of hairdress will emphasize facial faults. On the other hand, these same faults may be much mitigated by the choice of a coiffure that compensates for them. In the pictorial field, the hairdress may be made to give effective and startling emphasis to facial peculiarities that a portraitist would desire to subordinate.

Figure 25   Figure 26

The following arrangements of hair will make the face appear *wider*.

1. Hair covering the neck. If in a full-face view the hair is seen on both sides of the neck, the eye is forced into a horizontal motion in looking from one mass to the other. This emphasis on the horizontal causes the neck to appear shorter and the face wider. (Figure 25.)
2. Ears exposed. The horizontal movement of the eye in looking from one ear to the other emphasizes the width of the face in the manner described above. (Figure 26.)
3. Hair low on forehead. Hair combed low or bangs are frequently advisable with a high or bulging forehead but do not go well with a wide face. (Figure 27.)
4. Center part. This emphasizes width, and is consequently most becoming to a slender face. (Figure 28.)

The following arrangements of hair will make the face appear *longer*.

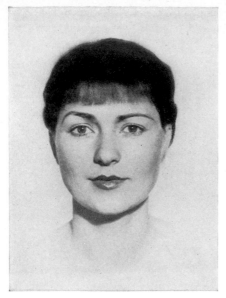 

Figure 27   Figure 28

1. Curved over cheeks. (Figure 29.)
2. Combed off forehead. (Figure 30.)
3. High side part. (Figure 31.)

It should be further noted that blond hair has a tendency to make the face look wider; dark hair, to make it look narrower. Therefore, the above-described expedients for widening the face are most effective with blond hair. Those for narrowing the face are most effective with dark hair.

In profiles, if the nose is inclined to be oversize, care should be taken that the coiffure does not place a knot of hair directly opposite. In such a position the knot draws attention to the nose and emphasizes its prominence. (Figure 32.) Similarly, if the chin is too dominating, it should not be emphasized by a mass of hair low on the neck.

If possible, advise the model against getting a fresh marcel or permanent wave before the sitting. A new wave is emphasized by the camera and always looks harsh and metallic.

Figure 29

Figure 30

Figure 31

Figure 32

Figure 33   *Figure 34*

If the hair is arranged in curls or ringlets, care must be taken that they are kept close to the neck. Failure to do so may permit the light background to appear between the neck and the curls, creating a disturbing white patch. This fault, which is akin to the "trap" discussed in the next chapter, is aggravated when a Semi-Silhouette Light is used. (Figure 33.)

The Skin.

One very real fault is not, strictly speaking, related to posing the figure, but nevertheless yields to physical adjustment in the form of make-up (which is more fully discussed in Chapter Eight). This fault is a *flat white skin*. This is very difficult to deal with photographically, for it lacks both crispness in the high-lights and warmth in the lower half-tones. The best skin for photographic purposes is a rather dark olive containing enough natural oil to give brilliance to the high-lights. If the model is afflicted with a flat white skin as described above, it is best to apply a very small amount of cold cream—not enough to be perceptibly greasy, but just enough to insure crispness of rendering.

Figure 35

Butchery by Light.

The whole basis of good posing is the exploitation of the plastic qualities of the human body, the clear demonstration of the relationship of its parts and their articulations.

By bad posing the structural relationships of the body may be concealed, distorted, or contradicted.

There is another means by which structure may be similarly outraged. This is *bad lighting*. Fundamentally good structure may, by means of harsh cross light, be presented as a series of violent elevations and cavernous depressions. A face may be cross-hatched with shadows until it looks positively mutilated. (Figure 34.) "Butchery by light" is not too strong a term to apply to such outrages. Mutilations such as these are not only perpetrated, but are often displayed in annuals and salons as examples of good photography.

Figure 36   Figure 37

The Basic Light furnishes a conventionalized rendering of structure. The Plastic Light, as its name shows, gives a fuller account of plastic qualities. The sharper contrasts of the Dynamic Light demand great care in their application, for with this light there is always danger of offending against structure*.

The Neck.

The column of the neck normally curves forward slightly. (Figure 35.) Tilting of the head to the front or the rear is principally accomplished by movements at the atlas joint (between the skull and the top vertebra), and does not affect this forward curve. This curve must be preserved in profile angles. A vertical neck gives the impression that the subject is in danger of falling backward. (Figure 36.)

Turning the head strongly to one side produces on that side of the neck (between the sterno-mastoid and trapezius muscles) a

*For a fuller account of these points see Pictorial Lighting.

"Anne of Cleves"   *William Mortensen*

Figure 38

Figure 40

series of accordion pleats which are generally very unpleasant photographically. (Figure 37.) Occasionally these folds in the neck may be made to contribute to the pictorial scheme (note *Anne of Cleves*, Figure 38), but it is usually best to avoid them. The simplest manner of avoiding these pleats is, of course, to abstain from turning the head too sharply toward the shoulder. This difficulty may also be met by raising the shoulder nearest the camera until the unpleasant wrinkles are hidden. (This expedient is more fully discussed in the next chapter.)

The neck is best displayed if the head is turned somewhat to the side. In this manner the long graceful line of the sterno-cleido-mastoid muscle is clearly shown. (Figure 39.)

In profile or near profile angles of the head in which the neck is made an important part of the picture, such as Figure 35, it is generally best that the head be tipped and turned slightly toward the camera. This best preserves the proper relationship between the head and neck. Unless the head is so tipped and turned, the impression is given that the face recedes from the camera, with consequent over-emphasis on the neck and jaw-line. (Figure 40.)

Figure 39

Two Ways of Dealing with Aberrations.

Two factors frequently unite to plague the photographer. One is the vanity of his sitters. The other is the unhappy prevalence of deviations from facial perfection—eyes that are pinched or bulging, noses that are snub or humped, ears that flap, jowls that overhang, chins that recede, and thousands of lesser defects. How to reconcile vanity and defects is a grave problem.

There are two ways in which faults and exaggerations of facial structure may be treated photographically. One is to compensate for them. The other is to accept and utilize them. The first procedure is based on flattery and assumes a certain conformity to conventional standards of pulchritude. As such flattery is a very frequent aim of the photographer, this chapter has included some suggestions for compensating for not too gross deviations from the facial norm.

But unless flattery of a fairly obvious sort is the aim, such deviations should be joyfully received rather than compensated for; for they will frequently be found to furnish the germ of good pictures. Aberration rather than blank conformity is the source of the greatest pictorial interest in portraits. The search for the revealing aberration must as a rule be confined to purely pictorial work, for the subject of a commercial portrait sitting desires principally and primarily to be flattered. Seldom does a sitter show the philosophical detachment revealed by Elbert Hubbard, who said of his grotesque portrait by Rodin: "This is the head of the true Elbert Hubbard, the counterpart of which I carry on my shoulders."

The photographer, unless his interest is mere standardized portraiture, will always be on the alert to take advantage of aberrations. In Figures 17 and 18 it has been shown how a round and chubby face may be compensated for so as to yield a more conventionally flattering likeness. But, by taking advantage of this very roundness and by emphasizing a dominant feature, and to a certain extent build-

Figure 41

ing the picture around these characteristics, it is possible to secure an amusing pictorial result. (Figure 41.) Both the pose and the camera angle serve to stress the very points that were subordinated in Figure 18. A final touch of exaggeration was added through "local elongation" by Projection Control*.

*New Projection Control. Chapter Six.

CHAPTER THREE

Shoulders, Arms and Hands

The Shoulders.

The shoulders are much more than merely the points at which the arms are attached to the body. They are, thanks to the articulation of the collar-bones to the sternum, themselves very mobile and expressive. They may be hunched forward, pressed back, raised, lowered, or rotated. Certain temperaments and races find their most characteristic means of expression in the shoulders.

Except in definitely stylized and formal portraits it is best to avoid placing the level shoulders flat to the camera. When the shoulders are turned at an angle, the one nearer the camera should be higher. (Figure 42.) Lowering the near shoulder (Figure 43) produces a very unfortunate effect, emphasizing all the worst details of the neck. It is often a flattering procedure to young women to somewhat exaggerate the lifted front shoulder. (Figure 39.) This procedure joins the mass of the shoulder to the face, and the raised shoulder conceals the evidences of strain in the neck that are apt to be present when the head is turned so far to the side.

The Arms.

The arms are so mobile and infinitely varied in their plastic possibilities that it would be an impertinence to attempt to give formulas for posing them. However, this very mobility of the arms leads to numerous common errors in posing them which the amateur should be warned against.

Avoid extreme foreshortening. (Figure 44.) Even without the emphasis that short focal lengths give to it, this distortion is generally unpleasant. The Baroque painters, it is true, delighted in such fore-

Figure 42

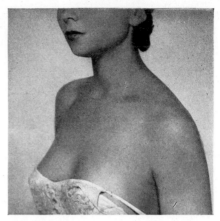

Figure 43

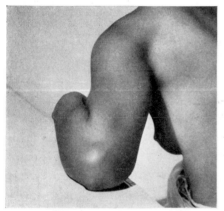

Figure 44

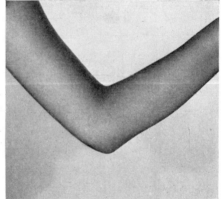

Figure 45

shortening, but they were able to present it in conventional terms unavailable to the camera. Furthermore, the sheer technical virtuosity of many of these pictures, rather than their beauty, is what makes them outstanding. However, there is no *tour de force* involved in getting foreshortening with a camera—a camera just as readily shoots an arm foreshortened as any other way.

Right angles should be avoided in posing the body. These are apt to occur between the arm and the body and at the elbow joint. (Figure 45.)

Figure 47   Figure 48

When the background is light, be careful of enclosed areas be-tween the bent arm and the body. (Figure 46.) Areas of this sort in a picture serve as *traps* that catch and hold the eye against its will. Because of being enclosed, these areas look even lighter and more aggressive than they really are. This is shown in diagrammatic fashion in Figure 47. Note that the small inner area looks definitely lighter in tone than the portion outside the dark ring. Actually the two are identical in tone. By using Projection Control, or other control methods, to lower the tone of the enclosed area, the offen-siveness of traps may be removed or greatly mitigated. Note that in Figure 48 the inner circle is much less conspicuous and apparently matches the tone of the outer area. As a matter of fact, in the latter diagram the inner circle has been darkened in tone.*

If forced, the elbow joint may be bent slightly backwards. This hyper-extension (Figure 49) is generally unpleasing, and its use should be avoided. The skin on the tip of the elbow is liable to be (especially with mature models) rather coarse and leathery. This unpleasant characteristic is more apparent when the joint is straight than when it is bent. This fault is apt to reveal itself when the back

---

*An example of a "trap" occurs in the author's picture Youth. (Pictorial Lighting, pg. 37.) The picture would be improved if the small triangular area between the right elbow and the head were slightly lowered in tone.

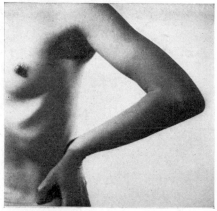

Figure 46

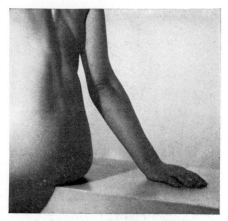

Figure 49

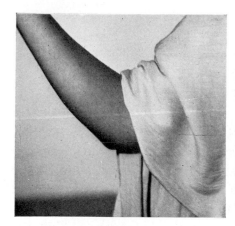

Figure 50

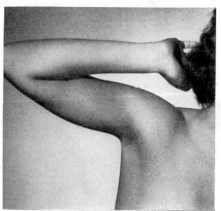

Figure 51

of the model is shown. (Figure 49.)

Avoid cutting the arm at the elbow by some other part of the body or by a garment (Figure 50), or by the side of the picture. It is sometimes permissible that the tip of the elbow be cut off by the edge of the picture (Figure 51), but enough of the arm should be left to carry the eye around the corner. Such a mutilation as that in Figure 52, suggesting that one arm goes out of the picture and another comes back in, is always unpleasant. Somewhat akin to this error is the arm that comes from the nowhere into the here. (Figure

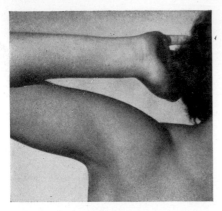

Figure 52

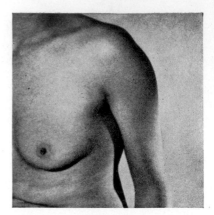

Figure 57

53.) The observer is momentarily in doubt whether the arm belongs to the model or somebody else.

The observer is subjected to a similar shock when, owing to the upper arm being hidden behind the body, the forearm appears to sprout weirdly from the abdomen. (Figure 54.)

An error of frequent ocurrence in posing the arms of a nude is the "stump". A stump is produced when the forearm is hidden, or nearly hidden, behind the upper arm. (Figure 55.) This position causes the flaunting of an elbow to which, apparently, nothing is attached. Enough of the upper arm should be shown so that the structure is clear and it is evident that no amputation has taken place.

Avoid any arrangement that results in the arms being crossed. (Figure 56.) In the following pages will be found many prohibitions of *the cross*. It is a harsh conformation, dubious in any composition, and, in posing the human figure, invariably ugly. The cross represents a raw opposition of forces, violent and inconclusive.

If the arm is pressed too closely against the body (Figure 57) it produces an unpleasant bulging of the upper arm. Generally speaking, any extreme suggestion of the compressible quality of the flesh should be avoided.

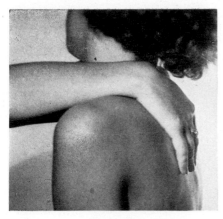

Figure 53

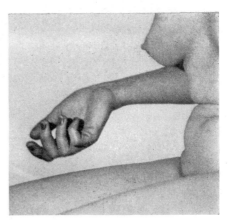

Figure 54

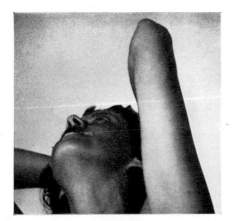

Figure 55

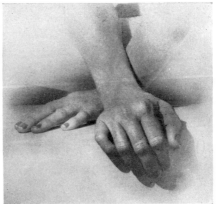

Figure 56

Hands.

Next to the face, the hands are the most individual and expressive parts of the body. Sometimes, indeed, when the face has been trained to impassivity, or has been made up according to standardized patterns of pulchritude, the hands may reveal a great deal more than the face does. Unrealized beauty may blossom forth in the hands, or a civilized-appearing face may be betrayed by hands that are lumpish and primitive.

The beauty of some hands has become a part of legend. The genius of Eleonora Duse was particularly revealed and is perhaps best remembered in the unearthly beauty and expressiveness of her hands in such parts as the blind girl in "The Dead City".

Such is its close relationship to the personality of the owner that the hand in primitive societies bears especial magic and religious significance. The particular virtue of the owner resides in the hand. Thus illness was treated by the "laying on of hands". And in England the "King's Evil" could be cured only by the touch of the sovereign. The qualities of a hand may survive after death; for in the Middle Ages thieves would burn the Hand of Glory—the pickled and dried hand of a hanged malefactor—to insure deep sleep of the residents of the house they were about to plunder. The hands are the vehicle of magical and liturgical gestures. Such a vulgar gesture as the "fico" still retains in Europe a certain magic significance.

In view of the peculiar importance of the hands, it seems strange that neglect or carelessness in posing them should be so common. Yet this neglect and carelessness is often met with.

A very frequent fault, and one that usually betrays the agitation of the sitter, consists of tangled digits. (Figure 59.) Even more orderly *clasped hands* (Figure 58) are apt to be disagreeable. The Romans regarded this posture as a hindrance to all kinds of business, and in council no man was permitted to clasp his hands. In a pictorial composition, these knotted or entwined fingers exert a similar inhibiting or obstructing influence.

The hands are such expressive members that we resent any pose that denies them this expressiveness. An utterly relaxed hand suggests either death or complete lack of individuality. Particularly bad are poses that leave the hands lying about in careless, accidental fashion, like blobs of inanimate matter. (Figures 60 and 61.) Also objectionable because of its flat unexpressiveness is a hand in which the fingers are spread fanwise.

The hands should be posed in such a manner that the individual digits are clearly defined. (Figure 62.) The hand is best presented edgewise or three-quarters turned rather than flat to the camera.

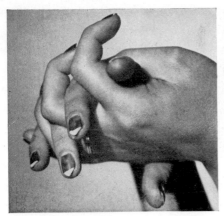

Figure 58

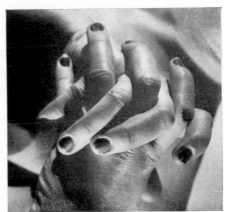

Figure 59

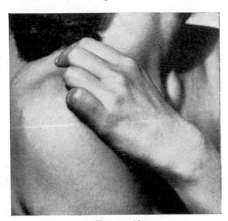

Figure 60

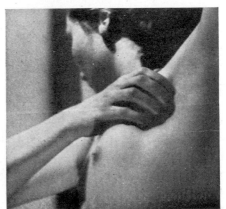

Figure 61

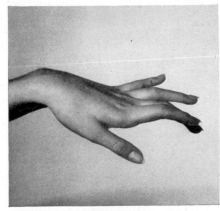

Figure 62

Figure 64

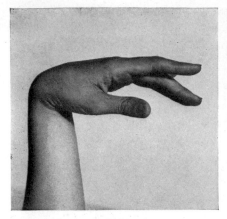

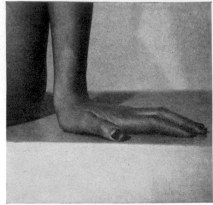

Figure 65   *Figure 66*

The edge or three-quarters angle much reduces the mass of the hand and at the same time accentuates its expressive qualities. Try to keep the hands separate and individual. Frequently this problem is best solved by including only one hand in a portrait. (Figure 172.) If the hands are allowed to touch, special care must be taken to preserve the individuality of each. Note in Figure 63, which is patterned after Durer's familiar engraving, the manner in which the problem is met.

With the hands, as with other parts of the body, good structure and arrangement are subject to *butchery by light*. Note the clear presentation of structure in Figure 62 under the Basic Light. Contrast this with the confusion introduced by the cross light in Figure 59.

The problem of empathy is involved when something is held in the hand. The strength with which it is held must be appropriate to the nature and weight of the object. Unless warned against it, a nervous model given a flower to hold is apt, instead of touching it delicately, to seize the stem as though it were a hoe handle. (Figure 64.) Conversely, a substantial object, such as dagger or the just-mentioned hoe handle, should not be held timidly or tentatively.

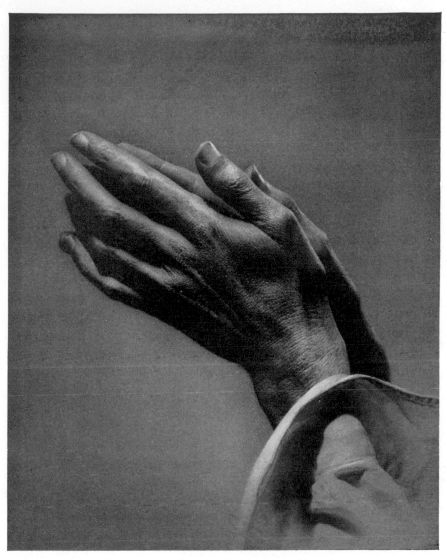

Figure 63

The Wrist.

The wrist joints are, of course, closely related to the hands, and are involved in any problem concerning the posing of the hands. A well-arranged hand may be rendered ineffective by an awkwardly turned wrist. There are several common faults that occur in the posing of this joint.

In the first place, avoid the *broken joint*. (Figure 65.) Excessive bending or twisting of the wrist suggests that a very unpleasant accident has taken place.

Considerations of empathy are also involved in posing the wrist of an arm that helps support the weight of the body. A collapsed wrist (Figure 66) conveys an unpleasant suggestion of inert and gross weight. The wrist posed as in Figure 67, on the other hand, implies lightness and vitality.

Avoid *cutting* the wrist, either by some other part of the body, by clothes, or by the edge of the picture. (Figure 68.) Such a cut is much less suggestive of mutilation if it takes place between wrist and elbow. (Figure 69.) An even better arrangement of the two hands is achieved in Figure 70 by eliminating the cross and merging the lines of the two hands.

A fault the opposite of the first mentioned is the absolutely *straight wrist*. (Figure 71.) The wrist is so delicate an apparatus, adjusted so precisely on its eight bones, that it should subtlely reflect every slight change in position of the fingers. Thus a straight wrist appears (especially with a female figure) unnatural as well as ugly. Where extreme masculine strength is shown, the straight wrist may be permissible.

When a gesture is indicated, the wrist should slightly lead the hand. (Figure 72.)

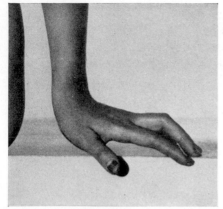

Figure 67

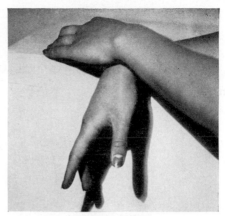

Figure 68

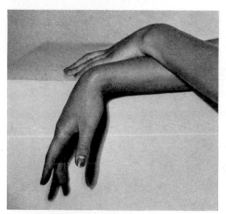

Figure 69

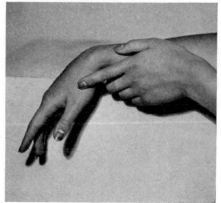

Figure 70

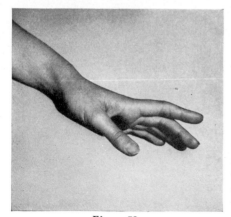

Figure 71

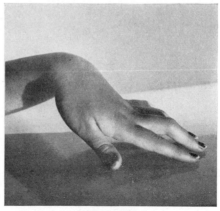

Figure 72

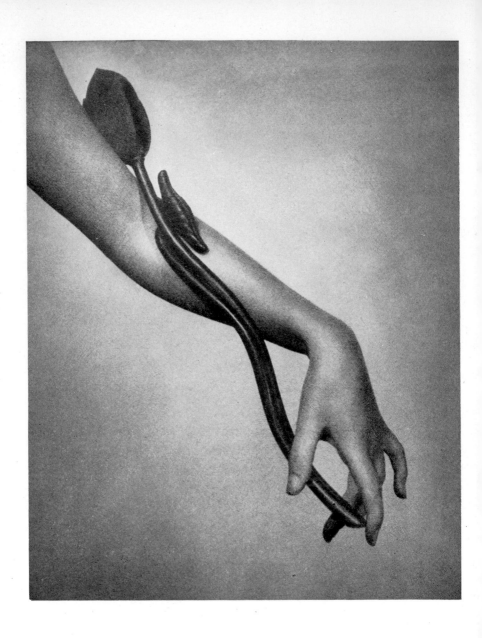

CHAPTER FOUR

The Torse

The torse, as described by Bridgman, consists of three major and approximately equal masses, the thorax, the waist, and the pelvis. The lower end of the sternum marks the line of division between the first and second mass, the navel, the division between the second and third. The upper and lower masses or blocks, i.e., the thorax and the pelvis, are fairly rigid and unchanging. The middle section, the waist or belly, is the principal source of flexibility in the torse.

This flexibility gives the torse a considerable scope for adjustment and alteration. Nevertheless, the dominating impression of the torse is massive and monumental. Artistic representation of it must maintain this impression.

The torse is the most beautifully plastic part of the body. Compared with this powerful mass, the arms and legs are mere expressive and subordinate adjuncts. Battered fragments of ancient statues, sans arms, legs and head, still have power to move us by the plastic rhythm and serenity of the torse alone. The torse is eternal, the face is incidental. The torse is the focus of energy, the very power-house, of the physical body; for it embraces the great nerve centers, the vital organs, the sex centers. It is inevitably the dominating interest in most nudes.

Both because of their plastic qualities and because of their significance as secondary sexual characteristics, the buttocks and the breasts have long been admired as the most beautiful parts of the female figure. A late Greek figure in the National Museum at Naples is known as Venus Callipyge, which, literally translated, means simply "Venus of the beautiful buttocks". Among more primitive peoples, steatopygy is often admired as a symbol of generation and fertility. This admiration is expressed in figurines and statuettes that hugely and grotesquely exaggerate these parts.

The female breast varies widely with age, race and condition. Certain of these variants are unacceptable and ugly for photographic purposes. Among the more beautiful variants, the following may be mentioned:

1. Probably the most beautiful type of all is the so-called "pear-shaped" breast. (Figure 73.) It is the type most admired in the Orient, as is evidenced by the frequency with which it is idealized in all Asiatic art. The pear-shaped contour is found in Japanese and Chinese painting, and in the sculptures of Ankhor-Vat. Rare everywhere, this type of breast is occasionally found in Northern Europe. Its characteristic profile is shown in Figure 74. It is high and full, and strongly convex on top.

2. The type of breast shown in Figures 75 and 76 is characteristic of Western Europe. It is not so full as the type described above, and is flat, or even concave, on its upper surface. Its most distinctive characteristic is the fact that the nipple is above the center of the breast.

3. The type most commonly associated with modern America is that shown in Figures 77 and 78. It is small, flat and compact, and generally accompanies a spare, athletic figure. It is interesting to note that the American type of breast is not greatly different from that idealized by the Greek sculptors. The latter is a little more globular in contour, but possesses the same symmetry and compactness.

Unhappily, the breast is at its best for only a few years. Increasing weight, and the relaxing of the supporting tissues, cause the breast to assume the characteristic lineaments of maturity. For this

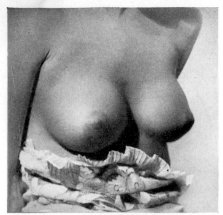

Figure 73

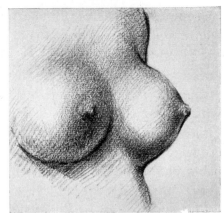

Figure 74

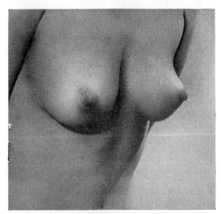

Figure 75

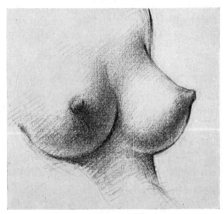

Figure 76

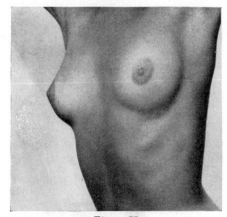

Figure 77

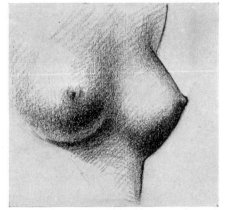

Figure 78

reason, a model is rarely acceptable for photography of the nude who has passed the age of twenty-five.

In addition to over-maturity, there are two rather frequently encountered flaws in breast structure which may unfit a model for posing in the nude. Sometimes the breasts are too widely spaced, with an unpleasant impression of muscular strain between them. (Figure 79.) An opposite fault is found when the breasts are crowded too close together. (Figure 80.) The latter condition is often accompanied by a bulging sternum (the so - called "pigeon breast").

The breast structure is very delicate and extremely susceptible to damage. Models blessed with good figures need to be constantly cautioned against dangerous practices. Most dangerous is the use of hard, tight brassieres. The only justifiable reason for a girl or young woman using a brassiere is for covering. To depend upon the garment for support results always in the weakening of the natural means of support. Many girls of eighteen have the fallen breast structure of a woman twice their age simply because they have tortured themselves with brassieres. Particularly revolting and barbarous is the practice in many boarding schools of compelling young girls to bind down their budding breasts with tight cloth bands —barbarous in the irreparable harm done to young bodies, revolting in the unhealthy complexes created in young minds.

Over-indulgence in certain exercises also may prove harmful to the breast structure. "Chinning" on a bar is especially apt to do so; for this exercise stretches and lengthens the pectoral muscles upon which the breasts depend for support.

Certain simple precautions should be observed in posing the figure in order to secure the best representation of the breasts. The model should be instructed to take a deep breath, at the same time raising the lower ribs. If sitting or standing, she should, *without strain*, hold herself erect. And, of course, *avoid contrasty lighting*. Much contemporary photography of the nude seems to be obsessed with the effort to display the breasts as protruding and three-dimensional. So harsh cross lighting is applied—with the result that,

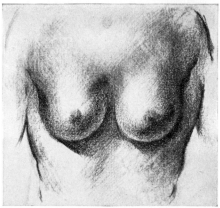

Figure 79   Figure 80

instead of retaining the delicacy of contour and the subtlety of modelling characteristic of the breast structure, you get something resembling sunrise in the Alps.

A Delicate Question of Taste.

A delicate problem (and one that must be met frankly) is that concerning the removal or retention of pubic hair in pictorial representations of the nude.

The old Post-Office regulation solved the problem in its own manner by arbitrarily branding pictures in which the pubic hair was apparent as "obscene", and by barring them from the mails.* From the point of view of the pictorialist, the problem is not so simply solved. Fundamental issues of taste are involved.

Indeed, good taste is the only thing that will solve this problem. A sense of what is fitting and appropriate will dictate the choice between removal or retention. Personally, I feel that in the case of nudes photographed indoors with emphasis on structure and plastic quality, the removal of the pubic hair is definitely indicated. Its retention creates a crass realistic note quite out of key with the subject matter and its manner of presentation. On the other hand, in

*Judging from the contents of certain annuals and folios that have recently been admitted to the mails, there is a present disposition to somewhat relax this regulation.

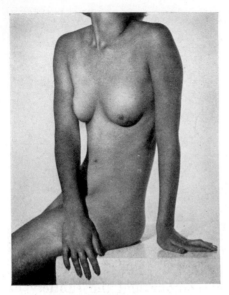

Figure 81   Figure 82

an outdoor photograph of a nude, surrounded by the open air, lighted by the sun, with emphasis on healthy flesh and blood (such as Dr. Grabner gives us), the retention of the pubic hair would seem altogether appropriate. Its absence in this case might well seem artificial.

Some Errors in Posing the Torse.

The massive plastic qualities of the torse must be preserved in arranging the body for a picture. The following errors, which are typical and frequently met with, result from failure to preserve these plastic qualities.

Twisting the body so that the shoulders are presented flat to the camera and the hips edgewise (Figure 81) produces a very unbecoming result with the female body. The hips are narrowed and the shoulders broadened thereby, with a consequent violation of the essential feminine contours. Since certain contemporary fashions are built upon this unfeminine plan—broad shoulders and narrow hips—it is perhaps understandable that fashion plates exploiting

Figure 83

these clothes should be so posed. But to extend this arrangement to representations in the nude—as I have seen it done on salon walls—is in the worst of taste.

When sitting, the model should always hold herself definitely erect. Failure to do so results in an unpleasantly *collapsed abdomen*. (Figure 82.) As this illustration shows, the breasts also are badly presented as a result of this posture.

In a three-quarter rear view the model's failure to keep her back straight is made evident in the slumped and protruding scapula. (Figure 83.) From this angle the body, unless governed and controlled by a firm spine, is apt to appear as shapeless and lumpish as a sack of meal.

The *back* is far from being the most interesting aspect of the female figure. As generally exhibited, it is a large uneventful area with few signs of structure. Yet it is extensively portrayed by modest amateurs who exhibit undue timorousness in coping with the frontal problems of nude photography. There is, I believe, only one pose

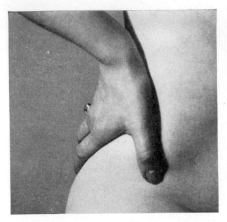
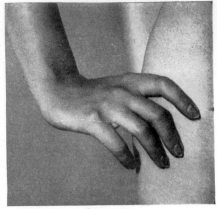

Figure 85   *Figure 86*

in which the female back may be really effectively presented. This is shown in Figure 84. Strength and resiliency are indicated by the curve of the spine. The two characteristic dimples assist the impression of firm muscular structure without loss of feminine quality. There is much likelihood, unless pains are taken to avoid it, that rear views of the torse will include the collapsed, leathery aspect of the elbows mentioned in Chapter Three.

A very frequent pose is that of the *hand on the hip*. But unless care is taken it is possible to go wrong in even so simple an act as this. Unless the intent is to represent a sort of washer-woman vulgarity, the hand should never be placed upon or above the crest of the ilium (hip bone). The hand placed above the iliac crest compresses the waist line and causes the hip to appear to bulge in a very ugly manner. (Figure 85.) The hand placed *below* the crest of the ilium, however, conforms with and delicately accentuates the curving line of the hip and thigh. (Figure 86.)

Carelessnes in arranging the seated figure leads to a fault which a student of mine has delicately designated as "the flattened fanetta". Normally the muscles of the buttocks are flattened somewhat by the weight of the body. When recorded, however, this condition pro-

Figure 84

duces an unfortunate impression of heaviness and grossness. (Figure 87.) In good painting and drawing this condition is never apparent, for the artist always restores the flattened curve. Photographically, this flattening and consequent impression of grossness may be corrected by directing the model to rest her weight on the thigh further from the camera. Under these conditions the roundness of the buttock is maintained. (Figure 88.)

A related fault may be designated as the "interrupted fanetta". This is apt to occur when the model sits or reclines on draperies, fur rugs, or cushions. Under these conditions it will frequently happen that a curve of the drapery, or an upward bulge of the rug or cushion, will interrupt or break the characteristic smooth sweeping curve of buttock and thigh. (Figure 89.) This interruption weakens the line that should be a strong structural element in the picture. If the curve is covered for any considerable portion of its length, the additional unfortunate impression is given that the hidden part is flattened.

There are many faults of body and face that may be eradicated or compensated for, but there is one condition that balks the photographer utterly. Many beautiful figures are rendered temporarily unavailable for nude photography by the presence of *bathing suit marks*. If these are at all conspicuous, even the heaviest applications of make-up are quite in vain, for the marks persist in spite of all efforts. (Figure 90.) If the photographer encounters bathing suit marks, he will, if he is wise, cancel the sitting and advise the model to take a ten-day course in "all-over" sun baths—or else make a new appointment for next December.

On the other hand, scars and marks of operations need seldom prove any obstacle in securing nude pictures. Unlike bathing suit marks, the actual area affected by scars is generally slight. Anyone with fair skill in retouching can readily remove them from negative or print.

Foreshortening of the torse—even to an extreme degree—may be very interesting and effective, provided the torse is exhibited by

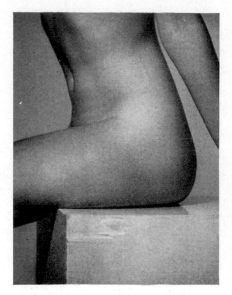

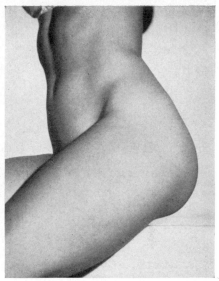

Figure 87

Figure 88

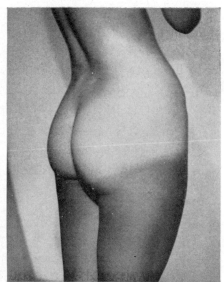

Figure 89

Figure 90

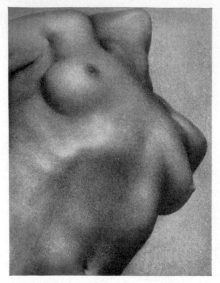

Figure 91   Figure 93

itself. (Figure 91.) However, when the foreshortened torse is contrasted with other *un*foreshortened members, the effect is awkward
and disproportioned. The draughtsman can get away with such
combinations because he is able to make compensating adjustments
of proportion. Note the pose in Figure 92, for example, which
would be quite impossible photographically. Attempt to duplicate
this drawing with the camera would result in arms and legs of in-
ordinate length contrasting weirdly with a squat and puny body.

The torse is particularly liable to *butchery by light*. There are
three pet tricks with lighting that are repeatedly perpetrated by
photographers who have more ingenuity than taste. These tricks
are startling, but they all violate the basic structure of the body.

1. The first of these is the use of a cast shadow on a white background. (Figure 93.) Everyone at some time, of course,
   has taken pictures of this sort. Unfortunately, they rather
   frequently get into salons and magazines. This effect is
   momentarily startling, no doubt, but commits libel on the

Figure 92

Figure 94   Figure 95

human figure. Note how the body and limbs are thickened
by the surrounding shadow.

2. Another pet effect involves the use of contrasty side lighting
    with a black background. (Figure 94.) This picture will be
    recognized, also, as a specimen of a type frequently met with.
    Note the strange parts of the body that are emphasized by
    this lighting, and that large sections of the body are com-
    pletely missing.

3. The third of these effects, also a familiar one, consists in cast
    shadows intersecting the body itself. These shadows (of
    foliage, Venetian blinds, tennis racquets, or what have you)
    create an irrelevant pattern completely at variance with the
    pattern of the body. (Figure 95.) The subtle rhythm of the
    body is lost in an obvious and mechanical pattern no more
    significant than that of a piece of calico.

CHAPTER FIVE

Legs and Feet

Owing to greater flexibility, there is the possibility of committing many more specific errors in posing the legs than in arranging the torse. With the latter, the most important thing is to understand it as a plastic, monumental mass; the legs, however, like the arms, fall readily into strange and awkward patterns.

The structure and inter-relation of the parts of the leg are most clearly revealed in a front or rear view or three-quarter angle. The beautiful relation of the inner and outer curves of the calf is best demonstrated in the front view of the leg (Figure 96). The straight profile of the leg is its least interesting angle and should generally be avoided. (Figure 97.) An exception to the latter rule may be

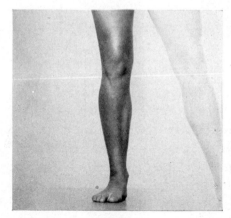

Figure 96

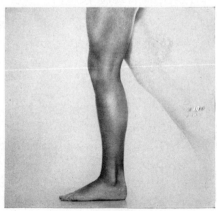

Figure 97

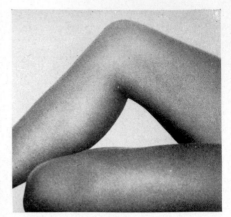

Figure 99 *Figure 100*

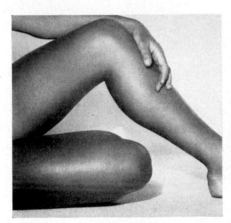
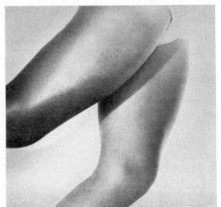

Figure 101 *Figure 102*

made in cases in which the toes are extended and there is a strong impression of muscular swelling. (Figure 98.)*

Reclining figures are often shown with one or both of the knees raised. Care should be taken in these instances to avoid *right angles.* (Figure 99.) This pose also incurs the danger of *traps.* This fault (as already described for an analogous arrangement of the elbow) occurs when the background is too light and the attention is sucked

---

*Note also Rope Dancer in Monsters & Madonnas. (Camera Craft, 1936.)

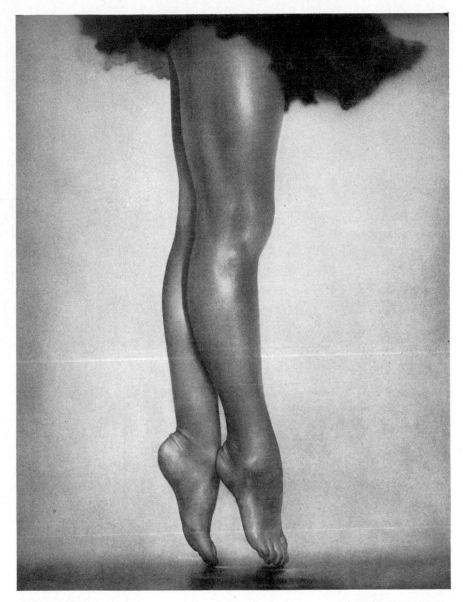

"Pas de Ballet"

Figure 98

William Mortensen

unescapably into the enclosed triangular white area. (Figure 100.) If a pose of this sort is required, the Semi-Silhouette Light should not be used. The Basic Light may be used; but it will probably prove necessary to darken slightly the trap area by Projection Control (or other control methods) in making the final print.

Elbow "stumps" have been discussed in Chapter Three. Equally unpleasant knee stumps are created by similar faulty arrangement. Bending the knee back and concealing the lower leg behind the thigh (Figure 101) suggests that a horrible mutilation has taken place. This is a frequently encountered fault.

Often the leg is cut by the side of the picture, by a garment, or by another part of the body. Never permit such cuts to take place at knee or ankle. (Figures 102 and 103.) When such cuts are used, they should be placed definitely above or below these joints. (Figures 104 and 105.) Another bad type of cut sometimes occurs when the leg is parallel to the side of the picture. If the leg is but slightly cut, as in Figure 106, the illusion is given of extraordinary width, because the mind is inclined to assume that more of the leg has been removed than is actually the case. In such instances, it is best either not to cut at all, or else to cut definitely and deeply.

The legs, like the arms, are subject to awkward and ugly foreshortenings. Seek, so far as possible, one-plane, two-dimensional arrangements.

When the weight of the body is rested upon the knee, it is liable, in a manner similar to the elbow under like conditions, to *hyperextension*. This is a very unpleasant posture, particularly if, as is frequently the case, the hyper-extended knee is contrasted with a forward-bent knee. (Figure 107.)

The *cross* is a conformation that should be avoided. It gives a harsh "X-marks-the-spot" accent wherever it occurs, usually at a point where such emphasis is completely misleading. Figure 108 shows a typical instance of this fault in posing the legs.

Crossing the knees when sitting is a permissible and frequently effective posture with smart clothes. With the nude, this posture is particularly disagreeable if, as in Figure 109, the near leg is crossed

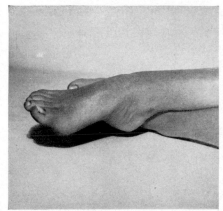

Figure 103

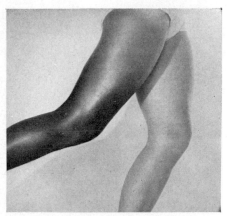

Figure 104

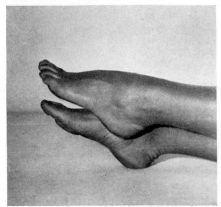

Figure 105

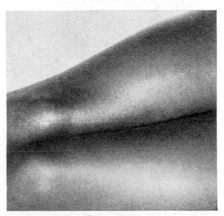

Figure 106

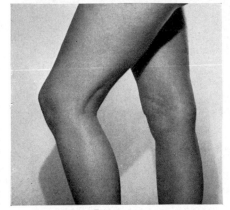

Figure 107

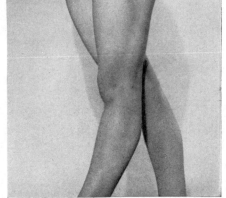

Figure 108

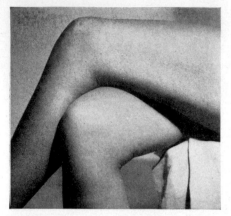

Figure 109

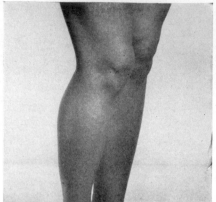

Figure 110

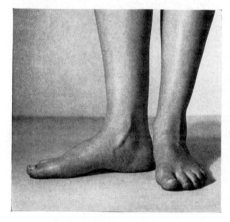

Figure 111

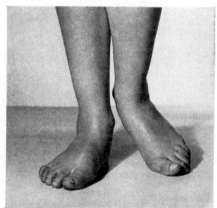

Figure 112

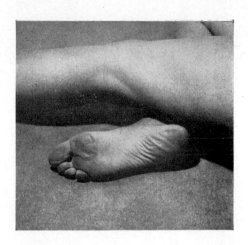

Figure 113

over the far one. Even with clothes, the arrangement shown here would be apt to prove unpleasant. The safe general rule is to cross the far leg over the near one.

Unless clear separation can be indicated, avoid parallel arrangement of the legs. As shown in Figure 110, parallelism without proper separation suggests heavy ponderous limbs. Such lack of separation is due primarily to faulty lighting.

Much care must be taken in placing the feet. As a general rule, avoid posing them so that they appear flat to the camera or pointed directly at it. One way they appear as great, broad flippers; the other, as stumps. (Figure 111.) The foot appears much more graceful in one of the intermediate positions. The apparent size of the foot is decreased by slightly raising the heel. (Figure 112.)

The soles of the feet should not be shown. Of all aspects of the foot, undoubtedly the most unprepossessing and least beautiful is the bottom. Yet recent collections of European nude photography have betrayed an unpleasant and unaesthetic preoccupation with the bottoms of the feet—together with the southerly aspect of the buttocks. Avoid the pose of the foot tucked under the thigh. (Figure 113.) The foot is apt to appear under these conditions as an unattached stump or weird excrescence.

CHAPTER SIX

Synthesis

In the four chapters preceding this, I have described and an-alysed the errors that may arise in posing various parts of the human body. These parts and the errors peculiar to them were considered as isolated and separate. In actual procedure, of course, the photographer has to deal with much more complicated problems than isolated elbows, ears or scapulas, and errors will be found to appear, not singly, but in groups. In this chapter, therefore, I shall touch on probable combinations of errors and problems relative to posing the entire figure.

Up to this point no effort has been made to indicate the relative seriousness of the various errors that have been described. An error has been simply an error, whether grave or slight. There is, of course, great difference in the quality of the various errors. Some are minor distractions, and some are major violations of the implica-tions of bodily structure. To avoid too great complication in grading the errors, it is convenient to divide them into two classes: (1) pri-mary errors, which must be avoided at all times; (2) secondary errors, which may be permitted under certain conditions.* Adopting

---

*For the sake of clarity, the author is here obliged to make an arbitrary division. With most of the errors in the list there is no reasonable doubt as to classification. Only in a few border-line cases has he exercised any dictatorial prerogative.

an ecclesiastical nomenclature, one may designate the first class as mortal faults, offenses against the structural logic of the human body, against good sense and good design. The second class might be called venial faults, offenses which are humanly inevitable in the course of the day's work, and which are excusable if not committed too frequently or ostentatiously.

For convenience of reference, I herewith list all the errors that have been discussed up to this point. The primary (or mortal) errors are printed in italics. Note should be taken that this list of errors applies in full *only to the plastic nude.* Costume and drama are not here considered. The use of costume conceals certain errors and introduces new ones in a manner that will be considered in the next chapter. Drama, as we shall see in Part Two, sometimes sanctions the deliberate introduction of errors for their expressive effect.

Table of Errors.

Head and Face.
 Split profile (Figure 4).
 Protruding ear.
 Cul de sac (Figure 7).
 Head tipped without compensating action (Figure 8).
 Head tipped toward camera (Figure 13).
 Head tipped away from camera (Figure 14).
 Head bowed.
 Profile head tipped back—banal (Figure 15).
 Eyes wrongly turned.
 Coiffure illogically shaped or proportioned (Figure 21),
  (Figure 22).
 Curl "trap" (Figure 33).
 Flat white skin.
 Butchery by light (Figure 34).
 Neck too vertical (Figure 36).
 Accordion pleated neck (Figure 37).

Shoulders, Arms and Hands.

Level shoulders flat to camera.
Near shoulder low (Figure 43).
Extreme foreshortening of arm (Figure 44).
Right angles (Figure 45).
Traps (Figure 46).
Hyper-extended elbow (Figure 49).
Wrist or elbow cut (Figure 50).
Arm from nowhere (Figure 53).
Arm sprouting from abdomen (Figure 54).
Stumps (Figure 55).
Crossed arms (Figure 56).
Arm flattened against body (Figure 57).
Spread fingers.
Tangled digits (Figure 58).
Clasped hands (Figure 59).
Casually misplaced hands (Figure 60).
Butchery by light (Figure 59).
Faulty empathy of grasping (Figure 64).
Broken wrist (Figure 65).
Collapsed wrist (Figure 66).
Straight wrist (Figure 71).

The Torse.

Twisted female torse (shoulders wide, hips narrow) (Figure 81).
Collapsed abdomen (Figure 82).
Hand above ilium (Figure 85).
Flattened fanetta (Figure 87).
Bathing suit marks (Figure 90).
Butchery by light (Figures 93, 94, 95).
Slumped scapula (Figure 83).

Legs and Feet.

Right angled knee (Figure 99).

Knee traps (Figure 100).
Knee Stumps (Figure 101).
Cut at knee or ankle (Figures 103, 104).
Wrong cut of thigh (Figure 106).
Extreme foreshortening of leg.
Hyper-extended knee (Figure 107).
Leg cross (Figure 108).
Crossed knees (Figure 109).
Parallelism without separation (Figure 110).
Stump or flipper feet (Figure 111).
Soles of feet shown (Figure 113).

The secondary errors all fill one or both of two conditions:

1. They may be adjusted or corrected by Projection Control or other control methods.

2. They may be tolerated at the time of the sitting if their correction would lead to fresh errors or to loss of vitality in the pose.

The primary errors fill the following condition:

They are capable of correction *only* at the time of the sitting.

A picture may be fairly effective even though it contains one or more secondary errors, if the latter are not too conspicuously displayed. A single primary error without emotional or expressive justification is sufficient to vitiate a picture.

Justification of Errors.

The retention of primary errors is never justified with nudes of the plastic sort. However, the violent quality of primary errors, and their startling contradiction of natural structure, gives them a dissonant expressiveness that occasionally justifies their sparing use in pictures that stress character, emotion and drama. These matters will be considered in more detail in Part Two.

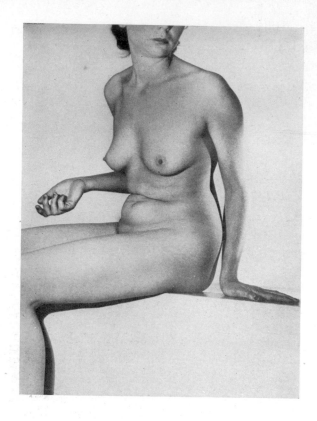

Figure 114

An Example of Combined Errors.

Frequently a group of errors is linked together in such a manner that correcting one will eliminate several others. Note Figure 114. This picture shows clear examples of the following errors:

Near shoulder low.

Arm sprouting from abdomen.

Arm flattened against body.

Collapsed wrist.

Collapsed abdomen.

Flattened fanetta.

Arm trap.

Undoubtedly a "slumped scapula" is present also, though not apparent from this angle. Of these seven clearly marked errors, five

94

Figure 115

are primary. The presence of any one of the five would be enough to spoil the picture. Of these errors, the "collapsed abdomen" is the worst, as it controls several of the other errors. Compare Figure 115. By the correction of the "collapsed abdomen" the spinal column is made to resume its function of support, the weight is taken off the collapsed wrist and the flattened arm naturally moves away from the body. The same action raises the near shoulder. The "flattened fanetta" is corrected by the model's resting her weight on the right thigh instead of the left. The sprouting arm is simply moved out of the picture. The arm trap is eliminated by slightly darkening the enclosed area by Projection Control. The revised picture, Figure 115, while no masterpiece, gives at least a pleasing impression of the qualities of the figure.

Figure 116

The four illustrations given in Figures 116, 117, 118 and 119, contain assorted combinations of errors. Concerning each of these the reader is invited to ask himself, "What is wrong with this picture?" in terms of the errors we have just been discussing. When he has listed the errors, let him then consider the most simple and reasonable methods of correcting them. The author's analysis of these pictures will be found in Appendix C.

These four pictures may seem to present outrageous and impossible combinations of errors, nothing that any reasonable person of good taste would indulge in. They *are* outrageous, but, alas, not impossible. *These four pictures have been closely patterned after prints that have in all seriousness and good faith been published in*

Figure 117

recent journals and annuals as commendable examples of contemporary photography.

Coordination.

There are certain generalized faults in posing the whole figure that are due to *lack of coordination.* Coordination is the act by which a pose, after it is cleared of its grosser errors, is given *unity.* There are of course two phases of coordination involved in posing a model:

1. Physical.
2. Mental.

1. On the physical side, *any* pose *tends* toward unity because

Figure 118

the body itself is an organism and a unit. The physical adjustments and the elimination of errors that we have just discussed are simply the means whereby the artist obtains a more nearly complete physical coordination.

It is of course to the advantage of the artist to utilize the body's natural tendency toward unification. Strangely enough, certain contemporary photographers seem bent on a perverse search for arrangements and expedients that contradict and violate, as far as possible, this natural physical unity.

2. There is a further coordination that grows out of the model's emotional and mental reaction. If the model has a clearly felt and conceived sense of the meaning of the particular project that is being

Figure 119

undertaken, he or she will be driven to a more completely coordinated pose through the unifying power of emotion. This emotionally unified pose is not, as a rule, pictorially useful unless the model has a sense and feeling of pictorial limitations. This means of co-ordination is, therefore, only available to an intelligent, experienced model of the "cooperative" type.* These problems will be more fully discussed in the succeeding chapters.

Coordination as Proximity.

Coordination is more easily achieved between elements that are closely related in space. If one arm points to the southeast and the

*Part Three, Chapter Two.

Figure 120

other to the southwest, and the legs are similarly distributed, the mere physical remoteness of the parts, one from the other, makes it difficult to relate and unify them.

From this fact we may derive and identify another error—the "error of outlying parts". Note Figure 120. The most conspicuous fault in this picture is the hand so far removed that it bears no sensible relation to the rest of the body. This fault is aggravated if the hand is represented as doing something or holding an object that is not clearly relevant to the other hand or to the general import of the pose. In Figure 120 the right hand obviously does not know what the left hand is doing.

This is an extreme case, but, unfortunately, not an uncommon one. A more subtle instance of this error is shown in Figure 121. The hand and arm, if not definitely "outlying parts", are at least near enough to the border line to make the pose seem uncomfortable. By moving the hand and arm merely a couple of inches nearer the body,

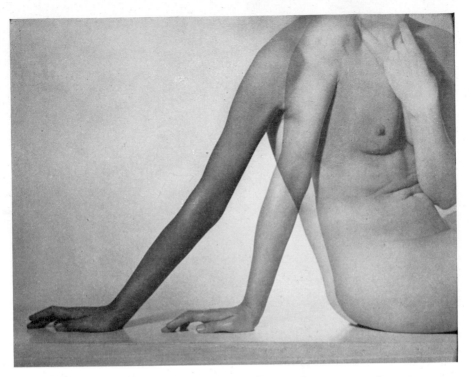

Figure 121

relationship is reestablished and the pose coordinated, as shown by the lighter image in Figure 121.

In this connection it is useful to remember Michaelangelo's remark concerning the design of statues. A piece of sculpture, he said, should be so designed that it could be rolled down a hill without sustaining any serious or essential damage. In other words, it should be compactly arranged, without any large projections or "outlying parts" to be broken off in the process. This same salutary compactness should be sought in posing the figure.

Stress and Strain

Coordination is also expressed as *balance of stress and strain*. The one great and omnipresent stress is the force of gravity, dragging

Figure 122

down and flattening all things. Opposed to this, and balancing it, are upward-thrusting muscular and material strains. In this uneasy realm of push and pull is found the substance of life and of the constructive arts.

Architecture is the soundest of all the arts because, more than any other, it is practically conditioned. If stresses and strains are not correctly calculated and provided for, the building will fall down— which is a comment more devastating and final than any art critic is capable of.

There are two general methods by which architecture solves the problem of stability and balance of stress and strain. Both of these

Figure 123

methods afford useful analogies in the posing of the figure.

1.   The first of these solutions is that afforded by the Egyptians —stability attained by sheer mass. The characteristic form is the pyramid, broad-based and as firmly planted as the everlasting hills. The same static stability is expressed by the more or less pyramidal composition of Figure 122. It holds itself up against the downward gravitational pull by the sheer strength of its mass.

2.   The second solution is that of Gothic architecture. The pull of gravitation is counteracted, not by static mass, but by upward thrust of vital energy. The drama of conflicting stress and strain is openly and actively expressed. This is the basis of the composition of Figure 123. In less violent form, the same vital resistance to gravi-

Figure 124

tational pull is represented in the "line of beauty" described by Hogarth. This supple contour characterizes natural growth and resiliency.

Another principle for posing the figure derived from architectural analogy is the *need of support.* Though modern methods of construction make it possible to build a balcony which has no external means of support, it does not look right unless some method of support is suggested. Similarly, in posing the figure, an overhanging composition cries out for support. However, in a picture the support does not need to be *actually* adequate. If the support is *implied,* it is enough. Note the overbalanced angle of the torso in Figure 124. In the finished picture, *Wind* (Figure 125), this is given the necessary support by extending the skirt.

"Wind"   ***William Mortensen***

Figure 125

CHAPTER SEVEN

Costume and Costume Elements

The Theory of Clothes

Man is unique in that he is a clothes-wearing animal. Anthropologists have established that there are three motives which have led man at some time in his remote past to acquire the quaint habit of wearing clothes. These three motives are

    Protection.
    Modesty.
    Decoration.

Much debate has been waged as to which of these motives was primary. Disciples of the materialistic school favoured the first; and Mrs. Grundy urged the second, maintaining (in the words of H. C. Flügl) that clothes were simply "a perpetual blush on the surface of mankind". Today, however, agreement is fairly general that, although the exigencies of protection and the acquired complex of modesty may have subsequently influenced the form of garments, the original motive for man's addiction to clothes was *decoration*.

And decoration is, of course, the one aspect of clothes with which we are concerned in this chapter.

Behind man's efforts to decorate himself these seems to lie an eternal inferiority complex. Naked man feels himself very small and lonely. So, through the decorative aid of clothing, he is at constant pains to aggrandize himself and establish himself before the hostile universe and in his own mind as an imposing and noble fellow with whom it is not safe to tamper.

This endeavor is made very clear in Emil Selenka's well-known classification of types of bodily ornament.* There are, according to him, two general sorts of adornment: Corporal (principally limited to primitive peoples) and External.

Under *Corporal* decoration he lists the following:

Cicatrisation (i.e., embellishment by means of scars)

Tattooing.

Painting.

Mutilation.

Deformation.

All these devices point to man's endeavor to make himself into an object of terror and wonderment to his enemies instead of the frightened bifurcated mammal that he really is.

Among the *External* types of decoration Selenka mentions the following:

Vertical—tending to increase apparent height. The Indian chief's feather headdress and the Senator's top-hat both come under this category.

Dimensional—tending to increase apparent size. In modern fashions a woman may wear a gown with wide epaulets in order to look masculine. Her husband pads the shoulders of his coat for the same reason.

Directional—emphasizing the movements of the body. In this class belong flowing draperies and streaming plumes that, borne backward by the wind, emphasize bodily action.

Annular (ring-shaped)—emphasizing the round contours of the body. Here belong such things as bracelets, necklaces and girdles.

Local—emphasizing a particular part of the body. In recent decades women wore bustles in order to stress certain feminine contours. Longer ago men were prone to give an exaggerated impression of their qualifications by means of the cod piece.

*Der Schmuck des Menschen, 1900.

Figure 126   *Figure 127*

In all this we see clearly man's effort to make himself out as a little stronger, larger and fleeter than he really is, and to emphasize, embellish and extend his bodily self.

Clothes and Anatomy

We have up to this point considered the body in its nude and plastic aspects. This is the logical approach to the problem of costume, for the necessary basis of clothes is, of course, the nude body. The exploitation of the body, not its concealment, is the true office of clothes. Clothes are a demonstration of anatomy.

In all the finest periods of costume design, there has been a strong consciousness of the relationship of clothes to the structure of the body. The structure is often exaggerated, sometimes in an extreme degree, but it is conformed to. In bad periods of costume design the bodily structure is covered up, violated and contradicted. Some of the very worst costume design on record appears in women's clothes of recent and contemporary date. Even the conventional attire of the Hottentot women shows a clearer appreciation of the basic

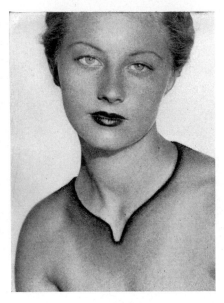

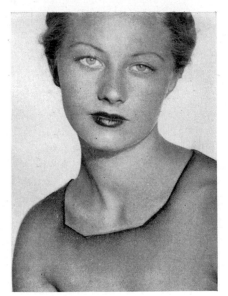

Figure 128   Figure 129

principles of costume than do some modern designs implying that woman is a flat-chested, hipless monster.

It is of course beyond the purview of this book to discuss at any length the history and principles of costume design. But it may be well to indicate a few guiding principles to assist the amateur in assembling the "Costume Elements" that will be hereafter discussed and in judging the pictorial fitness of modern clothes that he may have to deal with.

The basic principle of good costume design is, to reiterate, *Clothes should conform to and express the structure of the body that wears them.*

Therefore, avoid contrasty or emphatic patterns, for these will prove to be more pictorially dominating than the body they cover.

Hats are a frequent problem of the portrait worker. The contour of the skull and the planes of the face should dominate the pictorial presentation of the human head. Any hat is bad in design which leads the eye away from the basic contour as in Figure 126 or Figure 127.

Figure 130   Figure 131

The *neck line* is always a pictorially important part of a costume. The straight V-neck, although it appears in various periods, and frequently makes its appearance in modern clothes, should always be avoided in women's dress. This angular formation, abrupt and harsh, is strongly masculine in its connotation, and is neither flattering nor appropriate to feminine contours. Some photographers employ the V-neck in taking pictures of stout women in an effort to reduce the apparent size of the subject. But the V-shape is unbecoming, and frequently defeats its intent because the extreme contrast of shapes exaggerates rather than reduces the roundess of the face.

The modified form of the V-neck shown in Figure 128 is, on the other hand, very becoming, and quite conformable to feminine structure.

The square neck line is subject to the same criticism that has been applied to the V-neck—the shape is fundamentally unfeminine. If the corners are modified, however, as shown in Figure 129, this line

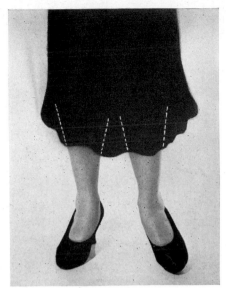

Figure 132   Figure 133

may be very becoming to a model with a finely structured throat and firmly fleshed bosom.

A curved neck-line is the most generally useful type in women's costume, conforming well to the contours of face and body. The shape may vary from a shallow oval to a deep curve. A strictly semi-circular neckline is not pleasant, being too mechanical in its connotation. Probably the most beautiful and natural type of curve for a neck-line is the *catenary*, which is the curve described by a chain suspended between two points. (Figure 130.) A necklace, of course, falls naturally into this configuration.

Avoid a neck-line that comes exactly at the level of the neck's junction with the shoulders. (Figure 131.) This point of separation is unpleasant, just as cuts directly at the joints of arm or leg are unpleasant.

I have already mentioned the undesirability of *cutting* the arm at the elbow or wrist, and of cutting the leg at knee or ankle. This

111

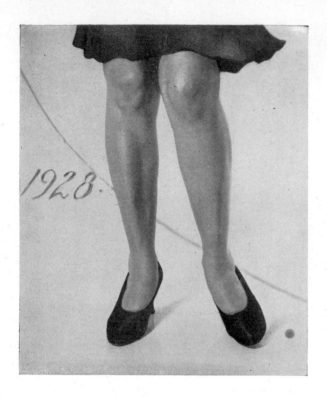

point needs to be stressed in its application to costume. The ugliest of all sleeves is that which is precisely elbow length. The elbow joint should be either completely exposed or completely covered. Nor should a sleeve come too close to the wrist. It should either terminate between wrist and elbow, or, in the manner of the Medieval sleeve, fall far enough below the wrist to join the sleeve with the hand.

In a similar manner, a skirt or costume should either fall definitely short of the knee (as in the Scotch kilt or the modern Greek fustanella), or else definitely below it (as in the classic type of ballet skirt). The worst of skirt lengths is at the knee or immediately above it. The knee structure, when presented thus isolated and unrelated, is fantastically ugly. Instead of knees, we seem to be looking at a couple of ham hocks. The days of 1928-9, when the world shuddered before the nightmarish apparition of one hundred million knees, were distinguished by what was no doubt an all-time low in costume design.

112

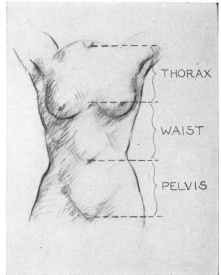

| Figure 134 | Figure 135 |

However, if the skirt is raised six inches above the knee, the relationship of the structure of the joint to the rest of the leg is again made clear and the result is pleasing.

The size of the feet is exaggerated by a skirt that is of exact ankle length. Either raising or lowering the skirt from this point obviates this effect. Although the dictates of fashion have prescribed widely varying lengths of skirt at different times, there is, between knee and ankle, only one length that is completely becoming. This length is determined by the curve of the calf. If the skirt is too short, as in Figure 132, the eye prolongs the lines of the calf with the indicated unpleasant implication that the leg dwindles to nothing. If the skirt is too long, as in Figure 133, a similar prolongation of lines suggests that the leg is huge. The skirt is of correct length when the prolonged lines of the calf are parallel or nearly so. (Figure 134.)

The normal eye level of the observer is of course considerably

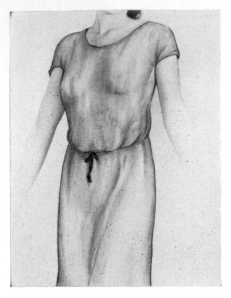

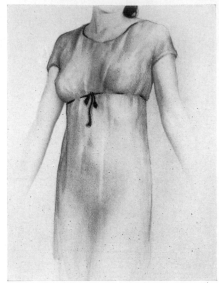

Figure 136   Figure 137

higher than the bottom of the skirt. This angle of vision increases
the apparent length of the skirt. To compensate for this effect, a
skirt generally is cut a little shorter than it is intended to appear.
The required amount of adjustment varies with the fullness of the
skirt, as the effect of increased length is exaggerated with increased
diameter. The camera, however, is frequently placed lower than
normal eye level. It may prove necessary to slightly lengthen the
skirt of a costume or sport dress to conform with this new angle of
vision.

The position of the waist-line must be related to the structure of
the body. As described in Chapter Four, the torse consists of three
nearly equal masses, the thorax, the waist and the pelvis. The points
of divisions are the base of the sternum and the navel. (Figure 135.)
In good periods these two points regulate the height of the waist-line.
The average and conventional level is that established by the navel.

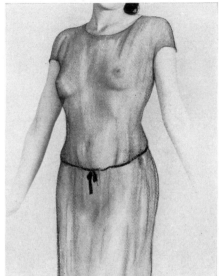

Figure 138   Figure 139

(Figure 136.) In Greek dresses, and in the derivative Empire style, the waist-line rises to the base of the sternum. (Figure 137.) In general, any waist level between these two points seems wrongly adjusted. (Figure 138.) Awkward also is a waist-line which encircles the hips and subtlely suggests that something has slipped. (Figure 139.) The oriental girdle, however, which crosses the back over the hips and falls in front to about the symphisis pubis, is very graceful. (Figure 140.) This form of girdle is felt as structurally logical because its lines in front closely parallel the groins.

It is interesting to note the relationship that exists (in good periods of costume design) between the level of the waist and the height of the coiffure. When the waist level is raised, as in Greek or Empire styles, the hair is piled correspondingly higher. When the low-hanging oriental girdle is worn, the hair is worn as flat to the head as possible.

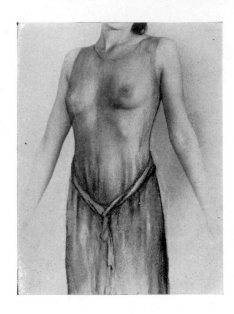

Figure 140

Folds and Drapery.

The majority of costumes involve the use of *folds*. These folds are the natural result of draping cloth over the body. Appreciation of the value and danger of folds is necessary in the assembling of "costume elements". Folds correctly placed are finely decorative. Wrongly placed and wrongly adjusted, they convert the best of costumes into a meaningless huddle of textiles.

Folds, when correctly used, conform to and comment on the structure and contours of the body, accentuating its movement and rhythm. Magnificent examples of the use of folds are found in the draperies of the Phidian sculptures for the pediment of the Parthenon. A similarly noble use of folds appears in Michelangelo's decoration of the Sistine ceiling. Note in each of these cases how the swing of the drapery conforms to and makes more impressive the bodily structure.

116

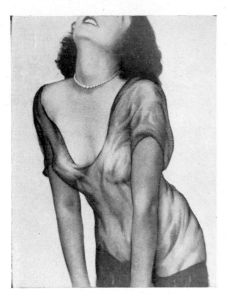

Figure 141   *Figure 142*

In addition to conforming to contour, the folds in a costume should also conform to the structural logic of the costume itself. It is logical, for instance, for folds to group themselves about the waist, where the costume is gathered by a girdle; but a cluster of folds half-way down the thigh would be clearly illogical.

The necessary relationship of folds to bodily contours is demonstrated in Figure 141 and Figure 142. Note in Figure 141 how the drapery conforms to the mold of the body and the curve of the breast. In Figure 142, on the other hand, the rhythm of the pose is interrupted and thrown into confusion by the erratic, meaningless line of the drapery.

A further precaution needs to be observed. When a fold appears in profile, take care that it is not too deep or too sharply pointed at the bottom. By a curious optical illusion, a deep, sharply shaped fold gives the impression that it cuts more deeply than the actual

Figure 143

Figure 144

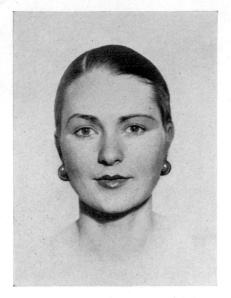

Figure 145   Figure 146

contour of the body. In the sleeve shown in Figure 143, the serrated folds seem actually to bite into the arm. This effect may be overcome by making the folds less deep and angular. They may be adjusted at the time of the sitting, or later by simple retouching on the print. The latter method was used in Figure 144, from the negative of which the detail of Figure 143 was taken.

Effect of Earrings and Necklaces.

Earrings and necklaces are not merely decorative elements, but, in a manner similar to the coiffure, they significantly affect the apparent shape of the face. For this reason they may play an important part in compensation of excessive length or width of face, or in pictorial emphasis on these same facial characteristics.

Earrings for the most part emphasize the width of the face. This is due to stress on the horizontal movement of the eye in looking from one ornament to the other. This effect of increased width is particularly noticeable with earrings of the button type. (Figure 145.) On the other hand, very long, pendant earrings are apt to increase the length of the face. (Figure 146.)

Figure 147   Figure 148

Among necklaces, the following designs are inclined to widen the face:

1. Choker type. (Figure 147.) The effect is more emphatic with round beads.
2. Short necklace with large round clasp. (Figure 148.)
3. Numerous short strands. (Figure 149.)

The following patterns tend to lengthen the face:

1. A strand of medium length with oval beads. (Figure 150.)
2. A succession of pendant shapes. (Figure 151.)
3. A few long strands. (Figure 152.)

"Costume" and "Wearing Apparel".

In an article in "The Mask" several years ago, Hilaire Hiler drew attention to the important difference between the two concepts "Wearing Apparel" and "Costume". The former is concerned only

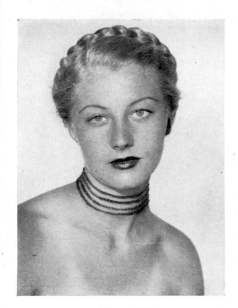

Figure 149

Figure 150

Figure 151

Figure 152

with material aspects of the problem: with clothes for utility and warmth, with clothes as a matter of ethnology, with the textiles and stuffs that go into clothes, with literal historical accuracy as to date and "period". "Costume", on the other hand, is concerned with matters of thought and idea: with the expressive values of clothes, with clothes in relation to gesture, with clothes as decoration, with clothes as an expression of national character, with the spirit and not with the letter of historical periods. Specialists who are anxious about the precise colour of Caesar's toga and the exact circumference of Queen Elizabeth's farthingale are dealing with "Wearing Apparel", not with "Costume". "Costume" is concerned with the ideas involved in these and all other garments, and with their capacities for emotion and expression.

It is from failure to make this important distinction between "Wearing Apparel" and "Costume" that many efforts in the use of costume in pictorial photography come to grief. With a rented costume of guaranteed historical authenticity the photographer goes to work and produces an excellent topographical map of the seamstress' art—but very seldom a picture. In Hollywood hundreds of research specialists toil at reproducing with complete fidelity the costumes of other times and other places, and the warehouses bulge with the fruits of their labours. But usually in the grandiose spectacles of the screen the costumes simply represent an appalling yardage of textiles, devoid of life and spirit and of any sense of the real *meaning* of the garments. The costumes seem a heavy burden that the sweating actors bear more or less patiently.

In the early days of my photographic career I worked several years for the largest costuming company in the West. Here, I imagined, would be found a magnificent opportunity to secure some real pictures. With eleven floors crammed with an almost unlimited stock of magnificent and authentic costumes it seemed as though one could not fail to secure something worth while. But during this period I scored practically a hundred per cent of failures. Figure 153 shows a specimen of my product at this time. (I also took about three thousand others, many of them worse than this.) Notice what

Figure 153
Costumer's Costume

has happened in Figure 153. We have a picture of a costume, in the midst of which there is incidentally included the placid and non-committal countenance of the girl who is wearing it. What the costume means, or was intended to mean, I cannot at the present writing venture to state. If the picture inspires any reaction at all it is the thought that you might lift the figure and discover a telephone underneath. Most efforts at using a costumer's costume of literal accuracy result, as this picture has resulted, in the complete swamping of the subject in the costume.

After producing several thousand pictures of about the same calibre as this, it became evident to me that access to costumes might be more of a hindrance than a help in the making of costume pictures. A costume that is already made is a fixed entity and is susceptible to very little alteration without damage. It is usually made rather as something to look at than to move in. Materials and patterns are frequently too conspicuous, and there is a tendency to use pictorially extraneous detail.

Costume Elements.

Though costume forms and mutations are many, the *elements of costume* are few and simple. Structurally, costume is merely pieces of cloth that are variously attached to and draped about the human frame. The seams, hooks and buttons wherewith they are attached or draped are mere mechanical details, of no interest pictorially. With these ideas in mind I began experimenting with *building up* costumes with a series of drapes—that is, working with costume elements instead of with completed and assembled garments. The method proved to be eminently successful; the drapes allowed for a large measure of control, and costume could be made both expressive and subordinate.

I found that a small number of costume elements would serve for almost all pictorial purposes. The list that follows has served for nearly all my pictorial costumes for several years. This list is offered as an example only. Differing needs will undoubtedly suggest changes or additions. The number of elements should not be substantially increased, however: a large part of the advantage of this method is lost if the elements are so numerous as to be unfamiliar and difficult to control. Actually, all the costume materials hereafter listed could easily be packed in a single small suitcase.

> 1. Two well aged grey monk's cloth sacks, torn and frayed around one end.

This material should be thoroughly aged. It should be washed several times to remove the sizing or stiffening and then hung out in sun and wind until it is well weathered.

This element has frequently been used to costume old men and old women. (*Wong*: Figure 194.) The frayed edge is particularly apt in suggesting the decrepitude of extreme old age. (*Daughter of Gobi*: Figure 154.)

"Daughter of Gobi"   *William Mortensen*

Figure 154

"*Lazarus,*" *V*   *William Mortensen*

Figure 155

"*Erasmus*"   *William Mortensen*

Figure 156

"The Outcasts"

Figure 157

William Mortensen

These soft torn rags are also used in *Lazarus V* (Figure 155). With the aid of a chain these elements may be made to suggest the costume of the Renaissance (*Erasmus*: Figure 156.) Poverty is, of course, the commonest connotation of rags, and it is for this purpose that these elements are used in *The Outcasts* (Figure 157). These elements are also frequently used as padding to build out the shoulders or back under other drapes.

     2. A dark yellow brocade drape of Italian design, one yard wide by two yards long.

The pattern in this element should not be too conspicuous. The colour chosen is rich and effective photographically. The material should be soft but substantial.

"*A La Gare*" *William Mortensen*

Figure 158

The brocaded pattern and the Italian design make this element particularly fitting for Renaissance costume. In *Erasmus*: Figure 156, for instance, it serves to suggest a doublet. With female figures it may be used as a rather heavy and voluptuous shoulder drape, or it may be pinned in front to form an elaborate bodice. When confused in folds the brocaded pattern may suggest the quaint, nondescript design of a shawl. (*A la Gare*: Figure 158). Or, reversed, it may be used as an outer dress or apron, as in *Woman of Languedoc*. (Figure 163.)

    3. Two pieces of black velvet, the smaller twelve by eighteen inches, the larger one yard by two yards.

The smaller one, variously folded and shaped, is used for Medieval and Renaissance headdresses and caps. (*Erasmus*: Figure 156.) A frequent incidental use of this small piece of velvet is to fill in the disturbing open triangle that occurs between the body and arms when the elbows are spread. The larger piece may be used for building a bodice or as a shoulder drape. It is also of sufficient size to be used as a black background for a head study when desired.

    4. An old fur neckpiece.

This is useful in adding characteristic details of fur to Renaissance costumes. Note its use in *Erasmus*. With a little variation, it may be converted into a collar, a turban, or a Cossack hat.

    5. Three scarfs of rather elaborate or even gaudy pattern.

These are used in small sections where an accent of detail is desired. Such accents should be carefully placed with relation to the structure of the body. These scarfs may serve for Gypsy or Oriental headdresses, for girdles about the waist, or even for constructing a bodice. Note their use in *Stamboul* (girdle),* or Flemish Maid (headdress) (Figure 159.)

    6. One woman's under-dress combining petticoat and bodice. Its colour should be just off white.

        One long-sleeved blouse of unbleached muslin, with a round, gathered neck.

These are the only two actual *garments* included in the list. But

---

*In Monsters & Madonnas.

"Flemish Maid"   William Mortensen

Figure 159

they are both sufficiently generalized in form and free from sugges-tion of period to admit of the extremest manipulation. The sleeves of the blouse may be tucked up or allowed to hang loose. The draw-string in the neck permits of further adjustment; it may be loosened till the shoulder is uncovered *(Adelita*)*, or it may be closely drawn *(Flemish Maid,* Figure 159).

With the addition of distinctive details, the long under-dress may be made to serve as the basic garment for peasant types from all parts of the world, oriental women from North Africa and the Levant, peasant girls from Central and North Europe, Mexicans and South American Indians. This garment was used for *Woman of Languedoc.* It has also been found useful for direct and simple por-traits of young girls. The round neck-line is very flattering and carries out the suggesiton of youth.

7.   Three grey drapes, each 40 inches wide and 2 yards long. These have served for skirts and have also contributed to oriental costumes in several religious subjects. *(Lazarus* III: Figure 160.)

8.   Three pieces of ivory coloured lace. Two of these are 6 inches in width and 18 inches long, and the third is 12 inches wide and a yard long.

The smaller pieces of lace may be used for delicate headdresses on women, and the larger one for a mantilla. They also may be employed in the construction of bodices of various periods and places. With the addition of a little starch and a drawstring the lace may be converted into a ruff for Elizabethan or Dutch costumes. The lace may also be used, like the scarfs listed in (5), as an accent of detail.

9.   Several items of hand-wrought jewelry.

Excellent costume jewelry for photographic purposes may be made from plastic clay and painted with bronze gilt. Useful items may also be gleaned from the counters of the "Five and Ten". The following list is adequate for most purposes:

---

*Pictorial Lighting, p. 77.

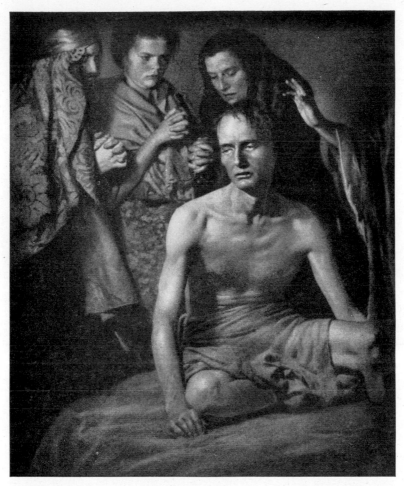

"Lazarus," III   *William Mortensen*

Figure 160

Two necklaces, one of the choker type, one long enough to make a double chain.

Two rings of good size.

Several glass bracelets..

Two brass wristlets.

Two heavy buckles.

One heavy gilt or bronze chain, two feet long.

This completes the list of costume elements. I have on occasion used numerous other costume items for specific effect—Spanish shawls, daggers, small "hand properties", etc. These are not included in the list as they are not sufficiently generalized to be regarded as elements.

There are a few purposes for which these costume elements will not prove of use. Military costume, of course, demands accuracy of detail: such accuracy is, as a matter of fact, the very essence of military costume. But accuracy of this sort is rarely pictorial. Costume in a picture should be *generalized* and *universal*. In creating a Medieval costume, for example, from the elements listed above, we do not strive to reproduce a particular dress that was worn in a particular place on a particular day in the year 1259. Rather the effort is to suggest, with as few elements as possible and with as little literal detail as possible, the general feeling of the period.

Using the Elements.

One who uses these costume elements for the first time will probably be discouraged by their appearance. Their colour is uninteresting, and to the naked eye they clearly reveal their miscellaneous origin. Learn to regard them *photographically*, in terms of greys and halftones. Examine the costume frequently, during the course of its construction, through the blue or blue-gray monochromatic structure filter*, and in the ground glass of the camera.

*A fairly satisfactory viewing filter may be made from the Pot Blue Sheet Glass which is carried in stock by large glass or chemical supply houses. Libbey-Owens-Ford Co. manufactures what is known as Dark Blue Plate Glass, which will also serve the purpose. These two materials cost from 25c to 50c for a four inch square. They are not completely monochromatic, but will give reasonable satisfaction in practice.

The reader will of course understand that the viewing glass or structure filter is used only before the eye to inspect the gradations of the subject as they appear in monochrome. It is never used in front of the camera lens.

Figure 161

In devising a costume with these elements, plan it in terms of a few concise and significant items. Lay out the elements you contemplate using where they may be readily reached. Build up the costume gradually, element by element. Take plenty of exposures of all stages: sometimes the simple earlier version will furnish a better picture than the completed costume. If any pose or expres-

135

sion looks interesting, take the picture, even though the costume needs adjusting. Frequently in making such an adjustment the desired quality will be lost. In the final stages, study the composition of the elements carefully in the ground glass, make numerous readjustments and alterations, and take exposures of all variants.

A couple of examples will show more clearly the manner in which the elements are handled. Figure 161 shows the elements used in *Erasmus* (Figure 156). They are:

    a. Yellow brocade drape.
    b. Two monks' cloth drapes.
    c. Square of black velvet.
    d. Fur neck-piece.
    e. Gilt chain.
    f. One buckle.

These elements were applied as follows: The yellow brocade was draped over the model's shoulders and left arm, the ends of the cloth hanging down his back. The two pieces of monks' cloth were laid over either shoulder and lapped in front to produce the V at the neck. The model then seated himself behind a table, on which he rested his elbows. At this point the draperies were more carefully adjusted. The chain, somewhat lengthened by a piece of string, was hung around the neck. The string was concealed under the fur piece, which was hung across the shoulders with the ends to the rear. Finally the black velvet, with the buckle attached, was folded and laid on the head. Considerable experiment was necessary to secure good design and interesting pattern in the cap.

A large number of exposures were taken, with many slight variants and minor adjustments of set-up.

Figure 162 shows the elements used in costuming the *Flemish Maid*, viz.:

    a. Blouse.
    b. Three scarfs.
    c. Two pieces of lace.
    d. Brocade drape.
    e. Jewelry, consisting of choker necklace and four bracelets.

Figure 162

The procedure of building up this costume was as follows: blouse was put on, with the sleeves tucked up and the gathe neck drawn fairly close. A wide scarf was tied about the hips. headdress was built of two pieces of lace and a scarf laid over head. With this much of the costume in place, the model seat herself and the piece of brocade was adjusted over her lap. Sever exposures were made. The arm of the chair was then partial covered with another scarf and the jewelry was added. More e posures were made with various arrangements of the bracelets an

s positions of the arms and head. Finally, to give point to her
e, the knitting needle or bodkin was placed in her hand. This
eality nothing but a twig plucked from a bush outside the door.
nall hand properties such as this are so integral a part of the
rial conception that they are properly regarded as a depart-
of costume. They are so diverse that they cannot be reduced
ements, but they can frequently be improvised from improb-
materials, as in the case just mentioned. Along with certain
is of jewelry, hand properties have the ability to sharpen gesture
to bring it to a climax. *Woman of Languedoc* (Figure 163)
ild be completely empty without the basket. In *Human Rela-
is**, note how the wristlet increases the power of the outthrust
n. A good costume is intimately related to gesture, prolonging and
phasizing the expressive movements of the body.

---

*Monsters & Madonnas.

3

"Woman of Languedoc"   *William Mortensen*

Figure 163

Posing the Clothed Body.

The advice and suggestions on posing which have been made in the preceding chapters have all been based on the nude body. The nude body is necessarily the foundation of clothes and costumes. Hence, in general, the clothed body is subject to the same restrictions in posing as the nude body. An effective and logical arrangement of the nude figure will also prove effective and logical when clothed. Compare Figure 163 and Figure 164. Note that the pose is sound, whether clothed or nude.

A classical demonstration of this close relationship between the effective pose of the nude figure and the clothed figure is afforded by Goya's two well-known paintings of "Maja". He painted her first nude, and later, in the identical pose, clothed. The effectiveness of the second painting is based on the fine arrangement of the nude figure in the first.

More freedom is permissible in posing a costumed figure than in posing a nude. Certain faults and details that would be obvious in a nude figure are frequently subordinated or completely hidden by the costume. For example, a full sleeve would probably conceal an "elbow trap". A skirt might hide a flattened thigh or a hyper-extended knee.

Nevertheless, in posing a clothed figure, it is best to work from the inside out, as it were. The right arrangement of the body should be established before details of costume are adjusted.

Modern Dress as "Costume".

The study of costume is important to the portrait photographer. It is possibly somewhat difficult to acquire the perspective that regards modern clothing in terms of "Costume" rather than "Wearing Apparel"—to revert to Hilaire Hiler's terms. But a portraitist who has accomplished this has gone a long way toward improving his product. He who sees clothes as something significant and decorative rather than something contemporary and utilitarian will no longer tolerate in the clothes of his sitters such characteristics as contrasty patterns, conspicuous detail, awkward necklines, and many such things that vitiate otherwise excellent portraits. The discovery of the "Costume" quality of modern clothes will greatly change his treatment of them. A derby hat may be made just a significant as a Roman helmet, if he knows how to go about it.

The pictorialist who is interested in costume will, of c   ʒe, familiarize himself with the subject. If he is wise, he will ʒ   ʒach it from the pictorial rather than the scientific angle. N   ʒstume plates, but the work of the great painters of the past ʒ   ʒd be his study. By these men he will find clothes treated, n   "Wearing Apparel", but as "Costume", not in terms of utiliʒ   ʒ literal likeness, but in terms of universal significance. And   ʒay with a clear conscience borrow from them in their handʒ   of such matters; for he will be but carrying on an artistic traʒ   ʒ that was old when they were young.

CHAPTER EIGHT

Pictorial Make Up

Not only the pictorialist, but the maker of portraits, frequently has occasion to deplore the quaint vagaries and apparent carelessness of the Creator in assembling the human countenance. The portraitist, whether amateur or professional, discovers early in his career that vanity is a phenomenon of more frequent occurrence in his sitters than beauty; so it often becomes his task to adjust the imperfections left by the Hand of the Potter.

In the Good Old Days it was the custom to make these readjustments by long hours spent over a retouching desk. The result of these sessions with knife and needle was all too often a smug and conventional semi-likeness of puttyish consistency. For users of miniature cameras such maneuvers with the negative are altogether unfeasible. For them, as for all portrait photographers, the most logical and easy method is the use of make up.

In the photographic scheme of things, make up is important as an additional method of control. As such it is subject to innumerable exuberant and tasteless misuses. But in capable hands it is a valuable aid to the pictorialist. Many an amateur has, no doubt, felt himself handicapped because a large variety of models was unavailable to him. However, with the assistance of make up and costume elements, a great deal may be accomplished with very few models.

In the history of man, make up has been put to two separate and distinct uses that should not be confused. One type is decorative and abstract, frankly non-realistic. This is undoubtedly the earlier, historically. It is frequently ritualistic in its background. To it belong such primitive manifestations as the face-painting of savages, and also such sophisticated developments as the make up practised by the Chinese theatre, by the Habima players and the Russian Ballet. The other, and more familiar type, is that of merely realistically enhancing or flattering the contours of a given face. The former type is intrinsically more interesting to the pictorialist, but to discuss it with anything like thoroughness would lead us far beyond the limits of this book. I shall touch slightly on its strange problems in the section on grotesque make up.

Four phases of make up will be discussed in this chapter:
> Straight make up.
> Character make up.
> Old age.
> The grotesque.

In dealing with these no effort will be made at laying down a definitive Theory of Cosmetics. Nor does the type of make up hereafter described have any necessary connection with make up for stage or screen. It is a self-evolved system, and has but one purpose —the most effective setting forth of the face in pictorial and portrait photography. It is specifically adapted to and designed for the type of lighting that I have described elsewhere* and will not work with the conventional contrasty type of illumination. Nor is it adapted to daylight use.

The basis of all make up is the bony substructure of the face. The facial bones of the skull, which do not change their essential contours after early maturity, provide the framework over which muscles and skin are stretched or draped, gracefully or ungracefully as the case may be. In every face the contours are dominated and controlled by this framework. Make up must always be conditioned by the fundamental bony structure of the face. Whether the make up is slight or extreme, whether it is realistic or grotesque, it must not violate nor contradict this structure. Whatever alterations are

---

*Pictorial Lighting. Camera Craft, 1935.

attempted on a face must affect only the fleshy parts and leave the osseous foundation untouched. It is failure to observe this principle that causes bad make up—flabby suet pudding faces with no more reality or substance to them than Halloween masks. Such a make up should be compared with an Oriental mask, which though grotesque in the extreme, has bone and gristle under its grimace.

Let us, therefore, before going further into the subject of make up, pause to meditate Hamlet-like on the grim reminder exhibited in Figure 165. The principal structural points to note in the skull are the following:

1. The frontal bone. Its shape varies greatly with different individuals, sometimes arched, sometimes flat, sometimes sloping. Its width is determined by the depressions in either temple.
2. The orbits. Note the large area of the face that they occupy.
3. The cheek bones.
4. The nose. Note that the upper section only of the bridge is of bone. The lower changes with age and is susceptible to alteration by make up.
5. The mandible, or lower jaw. This varies greatly in shape among individuals. With increasing age and consequent loss of teeth the mandible moves forward and eventually protrudes beyond the lower jaw.
6. Important depressions are found beneath the cheek bones and in the temples.

Study the skull well until you are thoroughly familiar with its proportions and structure. Note especially where the shadowed areas fall in Figure 165, for it is principally in these portions that make up is applied.

This may seem a morbid and bleakly anatomical approach to the problem (especially to that of such slight make ups as we shall at first discuss), but it is the only helpful one. Every face, no matter how lovely, is built from the bone out. A girl of eighteen has essentially the same bony structure in her face that she will have at eighty. The human head is not an egg, although I have seen

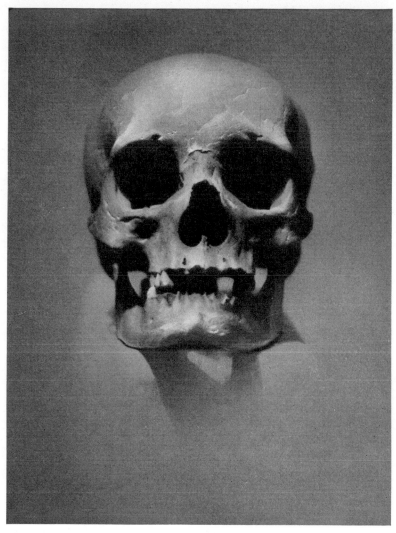

"The Basis of Make Up"   *Figure 165*

some retouched photographs that were based on the assumption that it is. One of the outstanding advantages of make up over retouching as a means of alteration is the fact that in applying make up the facial bones lie right under the fingers to guide one and prevent one from straying into illogicalities.

An artist in sketching a face roughs it in in the manner of Figure 166, which is simply a summary statement of the hollows and protuberances of the skull in Figure 165. Unless a face is constructed in this manner, solidity and substance will be conspicuously lacking in the final version. Figure 167 shows how the features are built up on this basis.

For the various types of make up discussed in this chapter the following materials are required:

> Powder in four shades:
> > Natural.
> > Light rachelle.
> > Dark rachelle.
> > Light sun tan.
> Dry rouge of an orange tint.
> Tangerine lip stick.
> Panchromatic lining colour (Max Factor #22).
> Lining pencils (black and brown).
> Cold cream.
> Crepe hair (brown, black and grey).
> Spirit gum.
> Cotton.
> Collodion.
> Grease paint (Factor's #26).
> $\frac{1}{2}$ inch soft bristle "bright" brush.

I have made the list as short as possible. Unless you do a great deal of work with make up, the materials given above should last a considerable length of time.

Straight Make Up.
Under "straight make up" I include such procedures as are

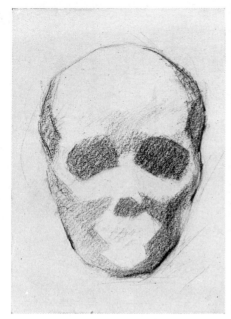

Figure 166   Figure 167

concerned simply with effective and flattering presentation of the
face and with the correction of faults without loss of likeness. A
straight make up simply accepts the face as it is and makes the best
of it. Nearly all portrait work demands some use of straight make
up.

There is a conventionalized standard of beauty to which the
majority of feminine sitters wish to conform. The frequent problem
of the portrait photographer is to bring quite diverse and unlikely
material into line with this standard. In solving this problem straight
make up is a very great aid.

The first step in constructing a straight make up for portrait purposes is to persuade the model to remove her street make up, wash
her face, and present herself "as is". (Figure 168.) Thus are simultaneously revealed the basic and inviolable structure and the faults

Figure 168
"As Is"

that need correcting. This girl presents an instance of the frequent fault of eyes that are slightly too small. This smallness is emphasized by the undue swelling of the orbit above the eyes, and the insufficient lashes. The mouth is interesting, but somewhat pinched in expression. Presented thus baldly, these faults tend to obscure the fundamental good structure of the face. Now, to correct these faults.

First, we darken the orbits with #22 liner and line the lower lid with the brown pencil. The lips are built out to a more becoming fullness with tangerine lip rouge. Figure 169 shows the extent and position of these additions. Notice that these alterations all correspond to the position of the shadow areas of the skull (Figure 165) and in the roughed in face (Figure 166). Then the shadows are reduced and blended with a finger slightly touched with cold cream, and the face powdered with the tone most nearly matching the natural complexion (in this case, light rachelle). The orange toned

Figure 169
Make Up Roughed In

rouge is blended from the nose line delicately toward the temples. Finally, the high lights on chin and forehead are slightly accentuated with cold cream.

The finished picture, "Ruth", (Figure 170) represents a conventional portrait job. The make up is small, but it is logically applied and simply enhances the best in the face without any loss of likeness. Ortho (green sensitive) film was used in making this picture. When Panchromatic stock is used, the #22 Panchro lining colour should be substituted for the tangerine lip stick.

It is of the utmost importance that the model remove her street make up and submit to being made up afresh for the sitting. The street make up is usually of the wrong colour photographically, and is illogically applied nine times out of ten. The make up given here follows the simplest and best known of formulas—eye shadow, lashes, colour on the cheeks and lip rouge—and yet in the handling of these elements it is possible to make alarming errors and to violate facial structure in a criminal manner. When the face is free from street make up the underlying structure is clearly revealed, and one may proceed to construct a logical and photographically accurate make up.

The eyes are probably the most important part of a make up. It is well to remember the art school maxim for painting that all portions that lie within the orbit (saving only the high lights) should be darker than the rest of the face. A delicate wash of shadow should be applied in the orbit. If there is a tendency to a swelling over the eye, it should be reduced with extra darkness in the shadow. When the model has dark discoloration under the eyes, do not try to cover it with light powder; rather make up the rest of the face in a darker tone to correspond to that of the discoloration. Thickness of the over lid is an especial mark of beauty, and if it exists it should be emphasized with a high light of cold cream or oil on the lid. In lining the lower lid be careful not to start the line too close to the nose: generally speaking, only about two-thirds of the lower lid should be lined.

The eyebrows need especial attention. Much control may be accomplished by the use of a brush. If the space in the orbit between the eye and eyebrow is too wide the brows should be brushed downward; if too narrow, upward. Eyebrows that are too thick and coarse tend to give the face a heavy, sullen expression. Their possessor should, if possible, be encouraged in careful and discriminating use of the tweezers. Thinning and arching the brows gives a better impression of the facial structure, and at the same time imparts added brightness and happiness to the face.

Coarse nostrils are a bad blemish and a difficult one to counteract. In such cases avoid with particular care all poses with the head tilted back. Red noses are an occasional problem that arises to harass the photographer. Liquid powder is the only remedy that I have found that will cope with them.

In filling out the lips avoid too harsh a tone contrast with the rest of the face. An orange toned rouge is best with Ortho (green sensitive) film, Factor's #22 liner with Pan. Keep away from smug-

"Ruth"   *William Mortensen*

Figure 170, Completed Make Up

ness and conventionality of outline of the lips. If the mouth is large, blend the rouge along the edges; if small, leave a definite outline. Thin lips should be only lightly filled out; piling on the rouge merely emphasizes the thinness. If the chin is weak, it may be helped with a high light of cold cream or oil. Never try to add a cleft to a chin that is naturally cleftless. Also avoid accentuating dimples or trying to add them when absent.

The rouge should be applied on the cheek near the line that runs from the nose to the corner of the mouth, and should be blended delicately outward and upward toward the temples. Keep it away from the line of the jaw. For added brilliance of the eyes, the rouge may be carried clear into the orbit. Rouge tends to increase the roundness of the cheeks, so on extremely round, moon-like faces, it is best to use no rouge at all. Blend rouge carefully: it must never appear as a patch or spot. Apply powder sparingly, always. Too much destroys the high lights, wipes out modelling, and causes the face to resemble a carefully plastered wall.

Once in a while the portraitist will encounter a model that from admiring but undiscriminating perusal of screen magazines has developed a make up that it is obviously derivative and imitative. (Figure 171.) It is generally useless to assure such a person that Joan Crawford or Jean Harlow has created her own definitely stylized make up only after years of study and experiment. The best thing to do with such a model is to concede her a few exposures and let her do her utmost, and then tactfully suggest a change. Usually when she sees the contrast between a logically developed make up and her own inept imitation, she will capitulate unconditionally.

Character Make Up.

"The proper study of mankind is man." In these words Alexander Pope summed up the thought, the strength and the weakness of his Eighteenth Century. In humanistic periods such as his, this intense self-interest of mankind leads to the creation of outstanding works of portraiture. Thus in England, the Eighteenth Century brought forth Romney, Reynolds, Lawrence, and numerous others whose concern was not with tricks of painting, nor with prob-

lems of Pure Form, but with human beings. So the artist in our century, which finds itself so curiously in tune with the crisp, prosaic thinking of the Eighteenth, when he turns to portraiture assumes often the manner of the psychologist. In our studies of character make up it must be remembered that the matter of ultimate interest is not the make up, but the character.

Character make up is not merely a matter of applying paint imitatively. Strict exactness of costume, literal fitness of feature, are of much less importance than the imaginative quality of the interpretation. Interpretation, not imitation, must ever be the end of character portrayals. To present Lucrezia Borgia as she might have looked *if* she had consented to sit for her photograph, *if* any photographer had had the temerity to approach her, *if* there had been any photographers in the Sixteenth Century, interposes too many *ifs* between the picture and its enjoyment. Rather a picture of Lucrezia

Borgia, since we are on the subject of that dangerous lady, should perhaps tell of the vitality of the Renaissance, and of the animal spirits, unscrupulousness, and opportunism of this famous family of "climbers". Or, if you were of a mind to follow the defensive interpretation laid down by Baron Corvo, you might even present her as a vastly misunderstood lady, of thwarted haus-frau instincts. Of course, the picture should not stray too obviously from known likenesses, but in any case *the idea is much more important than the image.*

Successful attainment in this type of picture makes considerable demand on the model. Mere physical likeness to the ideal subject does not suffice, nor is it even necessary. What is required is interest, intelligence and imagination. Acting ability of the conventional type is apt to be a handicap rather than an aid. My best results have been obtained with non-professionals, with models of the "cooperative" type, described in Part Three. The professional actor is apt to approach the problem from a conventional technical standpoint, and to impose his own professional personality; the result is affected rather than sincere, theatrical rather than pictorial.

The ability and qualifications of the model must always figure largely in choice of subject matter for character pictures. But given a model of flexibility and imagination, the development of picture material may proceed in two ways; from the model to the subject, or from the subject to the model. The personality and plastic qualities of the model may suggest certain character treatment. Or a previously selected character may be adapted and interpreted in terms of a given model.

In the instance illustrated, *Niccolo Machiavelli* (Figure 172), the make up plays an important but subservient part. Its function is to add a confirming touch of truth to an already established characterization. Something in this model's lineaments suggested attempting a study of Niccolo of Florence—he of the secret smile, obsequious and aloof, with sidelong mocking eyes that observed but did not commit themselves. When the psychological basis of the characteriza-

"Niccolo Machiavelli"   *William Mortensen*

Figure 172

tion was established, certain small make up changes were made in conformity with known portraits of Machiavelli. The eyebrows were covered with grease paint and drawn in narrower and more arched. The cheeks were hollowed by delicately blended shadows and added width was given to the cheek bones by small high-lights of cold cream. Rouging the lips for their full length emphasized their thinness.

Beards.

With all kinds of make up a safe rule of thumb is to go slow and use too little rather than too much. This is particularly true of crepe hair. The obvious falseness of false whiskers and mustachios is a matter of comic tradition.

Two things are necessary in working with crepe hair:

1. Careful study beforehand.
2. Careful and slow procedure during the construction of the make up.

Too many experimenters slap on a false beard with only the vaguest notion of what the genuine article looks like. So before going ahead with a make up, conduct a slight investigation into the life and habits of whiskers. Notice that the hair on the face grows in very definite patterns, and that it grows much thicker in some areas than in others. Notice that it grows in definite *directions* along the contours of the face and that it does not sprout directly out of it like corn out of the ground. Notice also that the colour of the beard is rarely a match for the colour of the hair of the head.

A convincing and realistic-looking beard must be actually *constructed*, a small section at a time, right on the face. A few hours before starting work, the braided crepe hair should be combed out and laid between the folds of a damp towel to take the kinks out of it.

The first portion of the beard to be applied is the part directly under the chin. It does not need to be so painstakingly built up as the later additions, as it is hidden by the rest of the beard; but it is important as a foundation. Apply the spirit gum to only a small area at a time, and let it dry until it is slightly "tacky" before pressing the hair firmly into place with a towel.

Figure 173
"June" Without Make Up

Apply the next portion of the beard across the front of the chin, directly above the jaw line. This portion should not be more than an inch and a half wide, and should consist of not more than thirty or forty hairs, evenly distributed across this width. When this portion is pressed into the spirit gum, another of similar size and width is added directly above and over-lapping it. With similar additions, the beard is gradually built from the chin upward. The adding of successive courses of shingles on a roof is the closest analogy to the process. The side portions of the beard and the mustache are built up in the same manner.

Avoid a sharp line of demarcation where the beard merges into the cheek. This is done by making the final "course" of hair quite sparse. A slight shadowing with lining pencil also helps to blend the edges.

157

When the beard is completed it may be combed and trimmed to the desired shape.

Old Age.

The simulation of old age by the use of make up requires a very clear understanding of the structural basis of the face. The haphazard addition of a few lines and crowsfeet (which is as far as many attempts in such make up go) serves but to accentuate the youthfulness of the face to which they are applied. Such lines are superficial and unimportant signs of age. What is important is the loss of flesh and slackening of muscles that reveal facial structure that was concealed in youth. Such changes are not necessarily disfiguring; sometimes a pudgy and insignificant face takes on dignity and power in the aging process.

Figure 175
"June" With
Completed Make Up

In characterizations of this type, imaginative co-operation on the part of the model is again demanded. Much more than the manifestation of simple physical tokens, old age is a state of mind. It is experience, it is resignation, it is weariness, perhaps, of eyes that have seen too much and of ears that have heard too many foolish words. Unless a model can suggest this quality, the best of make ups will avail nothing.

Proper choice of costume does much to carry out and strengthen the suggestion given by the make up. Notice in the picture of *June* (Figure 175) how the impression of physical decay is developed by the few frayed rags. In the picture of Lois Moran (Figure 176) (which is one of a series of character studies) the idea of frailness and utter decrepitude is carried out by the line of the dress.

In such make up studies as those under discussion, a feeling of complete reality must be created, no matter how much artifice is actually involved. A make up that is obvious is a bad make up. The type of make up that I am about to describe is a kind of painting in three dimensions. As the marks of old age are most clearly revealed under the Dynamic Light, the whole scheme of the make up is planned with this type of lighting in view.

In making the old age study of *June* (which is illustrated in its three stages), (Figures 173, 174, 175) careful study of the bone structure of her face was made, both by what the eye revealed and by what the finger tips discovered, so that the final result might be anatomically consistent. Then the skull depressions were shadowed with Factor's #22 liner, as shown in the second figure. Note, by comparison with the picture of the skull, Figure 165, how closely the second stage of the make up follows the bony contours. Half closing the eyes will accentuate the skull-like aspect of this stage.

Then the broadly blocked-in shadows are blended and the smaller lines are worked in. Remember that the lines simply represent shadows, and must give a three-dimensional feeling. In general, *blend the shadows toward the source of the light.* The major depressions should be given added emphasis by carefully placed high-lights. These high-lights may be produced by a slight touch of cold cream or by light grease paint. Don't spend too much time in developing small details. Work rather in terms of large masses and general effect. Step back once in awhile and view the progress of the work critically through half-closed eyes.

When the make up is complete, the unique and indispensable contribution of the model comes into play. In the picture of *June*, the relaxed muscles of the face accentuate the impression of old age, and the heavily drooping lids make the eyes look weary.

In making the final print, the various processes of Projection Control are frequently used with advantage. For example, in *Daughter of Gobi* (Figure 154), a certain amount of elongation was employed to emphasize the grotesque aspects. In the picture of *June*, local printing was used to intensify the illusive shadows, and, by

"The Seventh Age"   William Mortensen

Portrayed by Lois Moran

Figure 176

local dodging, luminosity was added to some of the cross shadows resulting from the Dynamic Light.

The Grotesque.

The word "grotesque" comes from the same root as "grotto", and is thus linguistically connected with the rites of deities that were worshipped in underground temples. Even today some of this subterranean connotation is attached to grotesque art. Though we acknowledge them less freely, we are still plagued with many of the primitive fears that afflicted our cave-dwelling ancestors. We have spread the light of our knowledge a little wider, but the outer darkness still swarms with dimly visioned shapes of dread. Grotesque art is a very human gesture of defiance, making faces at the great dark, thumbing the nose at the unknown.

There is a definite fascination in that which we fear. And in representing or contemplating the object of our fear in art forms we are able to obtain a release from its domination. Even the most determinedly healthy-minded of us are susceptible to the lure of the morbid: the unceasing demand for mystery stories proves this. The Grand Guignol theatre in Paris for years provided a steady diet of morbid shockers. Numerous modern artists have frequently expressed themselves in terms of the grotesque—Hogarth, Daumier and Goya. In the field of black-and-white, Beardsley and Alastair found the grotesque their most natural and effective vein.

The grotesque is a field in which photography has done very little. Yet experiments in grotesque may prove very advantageous to the photographer. The constant and hampering trend of his medium is toward excessive literalness. Work with the grotesque compels him to cast aside the props and crutches of similitude and likeness and to give his imagination a chance. Even though he subsequently returns to the tight chamber of Things-as-they-are, he will find it occasionally thereafter pierced with windows opening toward the unknown and swept with winds from beyond the stars.

The foremost exponents of the art of grotesque make up are the actors of the Chinese theatre. The portrayers of villains and demons in the Chinese drama have developed a series of highly convention-

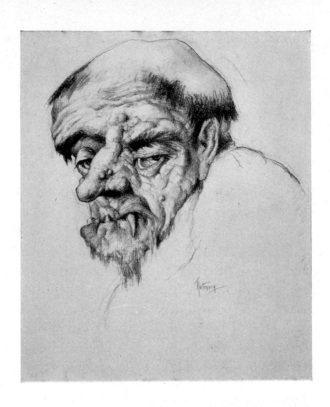

alized patterns of face painting, magnificent and alarming in red, yellow, white and black. The designs are traditionally established, and many of them are centuries old. Similarly traditional, though much less completely conventionalized, were the make ups of the characters of the Commedia dell' Arte of the Sixteenth and Seventeenth centuries.

Collodion Make Up.

In the motion picture field the best known exponent of grotesque make up was, of course, the late Lon Chaney. Rather close association with him in two of his pictures has placed me in position to speak with a certain amount of authority regarding his use of make up. He especially exploited the methods that I am about to describe.

The collodion make up is a difficult process and should not be undertaken without due preparation and understanding. I described the make up for old age as a species of *painting* for three dimensional effect. The use of collodion takes us into *sculpture.* Hence its use must be based on a sculptural sense of structure. Chaney's make ups were definitely structural in their conception. Thus, no matter how extreme they were, they gave a terrifying impression of reality, of flesh and bone. Never did they violate the admonition laid down at the beginning of this chapter that make up must not violate the basic bony structure of the face. To be sure, the structure was often tremendously warped or exaggerated; but it was never lost sight of or contradicted.

Rather than experimenting haphazardly with collodion make up, it is best to attempt a definite problem. Study the model's face carefully in advance and visualize clearly just what is to be done to it. A grotesque mask or a Goya illustration may serve as a starting point. It is also useful to experiment with sketches beforehand. Figure 177 was made under such circumstances. In these sketches, although you may improvise freely and fantastically, be careful never to lose sight of the basic skull structure.

One caution needs to be given before I describe the mechanics of the collodion process. The solvent of collodion is ether; so, lest you anaesthetize your model, it is wise to work in a well ventilated room with an electric fan going.

The major added protuberances are modeled in wads of cotton and tentatively fitted to the face. A coat of collodion is applied with a soft bristle brush at each point where the additions are to be made and the cotton is pressed into place. Speed in working is necessary, as the collodion dries rapidly. As each wad of cotton is attached, its outstanding fluffy edges are pressed down to the face with the collodion filled brush. After all the wads are attached to the face, their modelling is adjusted with the fingers. If additional protuberance is needed, it is built onto the cotton already in place with more collodion. With small wisps of cotton, each brushed into place with collodion, the modelling is refined and the large wads are blended into the contours of the face.

In the illustrated instance, *The Possessed* (Figure 178), the

"*The Possessed*"   *William Mortensen*

Figure 178

brow was built out large and heavy over the eyes. The nose was built up to meet the line of the brow and was somewhat widened. Additional width was given to the cheek bones, and sundry warts and excrescences were attached. The flabby folds of the neck were also constructed of collodion. Two turkey quills served for the tusks. Collodion and cotton were similarly used in converting the hand into a claw. The long nails were shaped from pieces of old film, and were tied to the fingers before the cotton was applied.*

After the cotton is attached and modelled to the desired shape, it is varnished with several coats of collodion. When the collodion is dry, grease paint is applied over the entire face. Considerable care is needed in working the paint over the attached cotton. It is necessary to apply the paint quite heavily, owing to the different colour of the cotton and the flesh. After a smooth coat of paint has been applied, it is usually necessary to emphasize the eyes and to accentuate the modelling with the lining pencil.

In photographing such a make up, the Dynamic type of lighting is used in order to give the maximum emphasis to the crude rugged modelling.

Body Make Up.

For the most part, make up is a problem of the face only. But occasionally other parts of the body are involved, or even the whole body.

Some workers, when photographing nudes, required the model to cover herself all over with liquid whiting. This was my own practice in my early experiments with the nude. But I soon abandoned the use of whiting when I learned that it gave very flat and dead results, lacking crispness in the high-lights and gradation in the shadows.

The use of whiting on the body, then, should be avoided. Rather the model should touch up her body with the smallest possible amount of cold cream. This gives a healthy sheen to the skin and imparts crisp brilliance to the high-lights. Figure 179 demon-

---

*Another example of collodion make up may be found in the picture Belphegor in Monsters & Madonnas.

Figure 179

strates the use of cold cream for this purpose.

This procedure is also useful in photographing a subject in a low cut gown. The usual practice of women, when they are so dressed, is to carry their powder down over the throat and onto the bosom. However, a very sparing application of cold cream will give a much rounder and fuller rendering of these parts.

Note that I have stipulated cold cream (*not* oil), and in infinitesimal amounts. Cold cream imparts a natural soft sheen to the skin; oil shines and glitters. A few years ago there was an epidemic of greased nudes, and one still occasionally meets examples of this unpleasant and freakish effect. (Figure 180.) This is an instance of the "Nujol nude", which will be discussed in Part Three. Observe that the high-lights are harsh and unnatural, and that they appear mostly in the wrong places.

It is sometimes required, for pictorial effect, to darken the model's entire body. For this purpose "Bol-Armenia" or a prepared liquid body make up is used. The Bol-Armenia is a powder which must be stirred up with water before using. Great care must be taken with body make up to apply it sparingly and smoothly. With

Figure 180

this type of make up the skin dries to a flat matt texture and consequently requires to be touched up with a little cold cream in the
high-lights.*

Make Up and the Hair.

As noted in Chapter Two, the arrangement of the hair may considerably affect the apparent shape of the face. Hair arrangement
is closely related to problems of make up. By using the hair to
emphasize, rather than to compensate for, unusual facial contours,
interesting pictorial effects are secured. In *Victoria Rebecca* (Figure
181), the already considerable length of the face is exaggerated by
the high coiffure.

By suggestion hair may contribute much to the general impression of the make up. Note, in this connection, the character of the
hair in *Daughter of Gobi* (Figure 154) and in *June* (Figure 175).
Observe also in *Belphegor** how greatly the bristly rendering of the

---

*It is well to emphasize again that body make up is of no use in counteracting bathing suit
marks. The marks will show through on the picture no matter how thick the make up is plastered on.

**In Monsters & Madonnas.

Figure 181

hair adds to the impression of bestiality.

Anne of Cleves (Figure 38) makes use of an interesting expedient in make up. Although she here appears as a blonde, this model actually has dark hair. The following procedure was employed. Her hair was first thoroughly covered with glycerine. Then powdered aluminum was lightly dusted on. Additional emphasis in the highlights was secured by a little more aluminum.

The use of glycerine with this make up is most necessary. It causes the powder to cling to the hair and insures its washing out readily. Without the glycerine the aluminum settles to the scalp, where it forms a stubborn crust very dangerous to the hair.

Hair that is dull and lacking in high-lights may be with advantage touched up slightly with cold cream. This was done in Figure 179. The same care must be here observed as in using cold cream on the body to apply it very sparingly.

An Admonition.

Make up is an exceedingly tricky and risky business, and very few people have the instinct for its photographic use. Only by a long process of trial and error is it possible to arrive at a firm working knowledge of this subject. The trials may be many and the errors horrible, without doubt; but study and analyse your failures —and then unceremoniously drop them in the waste basket. Not until you have the process well in hand should you exhibit any of the results to your model or to your public, large or small. Don't leap immediately to ambitious and grotesque extremes; the first test is the ability to construct a completely natural looking *straight* make up. When you have gained this ability you will have definitely added to your range of photographic control.

PART TWO

The Model As An Expressive Element

"Being" and "Meaning".

In Part One we considered the model merely as *form*, without any meaning beyond the fact that it was a human body. Form—firm, substantial and well-organized—is essential in all pictures; but form without meaning is mere geometry. Mere graceful attitudes assumed by the model do not create pictures. There must be *meaning* beyond the mere physical fact of the model and beyond the conformation of her limbs and body. A model as part of a picture not only *is* but *means* something.*

Herein we find the fatal lack of much contemporary photography, its shallowness and topical quality. We are stopped short by the simple objective fact of the picture, by its mere "is-ness". Beyond this, we can find no *meaning*. The "is" quality of the picture may be, and often is, immediately startling, like a skyrocket, but it commands no respect and no second glance. An accurate photographic tally of the bristles on a pig's snout or a literal representation of how a nude woman looks when she is folded into a washtub may gratify curiosity, scientific or otherwise; but then one turns the page and says "So what?" Such pictures mean nothing, they express nothing.

*There are, of course, other expressive elements in a picture—colour, notan, tone relation, lighting, composition, etc.—but for the purposes of this book we limit ourselves solely to the expressive qualities of the model.

The Emotional Fallacy.

"Expression" rather than "emotion" is the key to the model's function. There is a tendency to over-emphasize the importance of emotion in art. We are even told categorically that "all art is emotion". Emotion is a very misleading criterion. It implies that the more emotion there is, the more art. By this standard, a pulp magazine is finer art than the Iliad, and a notification that you have won the Irish Sweepstakes is an absolute masterpiece of literature. For sheer emotional power, art cannot compete with reality and every-day life. As Leo Stein pointed out, a bloody traffic accident in the street in front of an art museum will instantly empty the building of all those who have been supposedly "wrapped up" in art. But—and here is the significant point—when they have counted the casualties, and stared at the ambulances, they will all return to the building and to the *permanent* interest that art affords them. The street accident simply *is* for the moment: it is gripping, charged with emotion—and altogether transitory. But in art there is meaning behind the surface fact, meaning that is there today, tomorrow. and all the days after tomorrow.

The effort to reduce art to an emotional basis quickly comes to grief over the fact that emotion is often very vague, and even altogether lacking, in many great works of art. He would be bold indeed who tried to define the *specific* emotional quality of, say the Mona Lisa, the Venus of Melos, or the Taj Mahal. Some works of art, like the Egyptian sculptures of the Old Kingdom, owe their huge strength to their complete purgation from all such transitory human trivialities as emotion.

To be sure, emotion is frequently the thing that is expressed in a picture—and this fact is, no doubt, the cause of the tendency to over-emphasize the importance of emotion as a pictorial element. Emotion may be expressed, or the utter lack of it may be expressed; but the only important fact is that of *expression*.

The model, then, as an expressive element, is not important for what he or she *is*, but for what he or she *says* through the medium of the picture. And the artist's problem is to clarify *meanings* by means of physical adjustments.

The Method of Expression.

A picture is not made for the benefit of the photographer or of the model, but for the benefit of the ultimate consumer—the man who some time later looks at it. For the sake of the ultimate consumer, the model's method of expression must be a comprehensible language. The photographer may know what is meant, the model may know what is meant; but unless the man who looks at the picture can, by the mere act of looking, know what is meant—the picture has failed of its mission.

Thoughts and emotions cannot be photographed, despite the protestations of some mystically minded portraitists. What *can* be photographed are the *physical manifestations* of thoughts and emotions. Physical fact is ultimately the sole pictorial material. But expression is not achieved by the unselective recording of the physical fact. For, unfortunately, these physical manifestations of thoughts and emotions are not actually clearly marked or differentiated. Pictorially, a man laboring under a crushing sorrow might appear to be merely peevish. The camera would probably detect little difference in facial expression between a man who is plotting a murder and one who is figuring out another way he might have played last night's bridge hand. And it is regrettably difficult for the candid camera to distinguish impulses emanating from the spirit from those proceeding from the viscera.

The physical fact must be translated into the pictorial language before it becomes intelligible. The pictorial language of expression takes the form of *pantomimic symbols.* I call it pantomimic because of its relation to the ancient universal art of pantomime which translated thought into physical movement and attitude by means of standardized and stylized gesture. I call it symbolic because it deals, not with the thought or emotion itself, but with a sort of counter or chip that conveniently, concisely and unmistakably represents the thing it stands for. The pantomimic symbols of pictorial

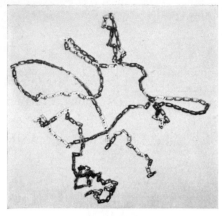

Figure 182   Figure 183

art are adapted to the peculiar limitations of the medium.

Let it be clearly understood: by "pantomimic symbols" I do *not* mean banal gestures. The very banality of these gestures is due to the fact that they try to compromise with the realism of physical fact and are empty of expressive quality.

The part played by the model as an expressive element is perhaps more clearly indicated by the three illustrations in Figures 182, 183, and 184. In Figure 182 is shown a length of chain, inert, shapeless, and without significance. In Figures 183 and 184 the chain, by the physical manipulations of the "artist", is moulded into two shapes of diverse meaning. The shapes are expressive because they are symbols: they *are* not "love" and "hate", but they *mean* "love" and "hate".

We are now in a position to deal with the frequently asked question of whether the model should *feel* the emotion that he or she is expressing. This question is analogous to the ancient stage controversy whether an actor need "feel" the part he plays. Representing one side of the controversy was Macready, who so depended on the impulse given him by a personal emotion that he was prone to excite himself before going on to play an emotional scene, by violently shaking a ladder that stood in the wings. The other side is

Figure 184

represented by the French tragedian Talma who would one moment be jesting with friends in the wings and a moment later in the midst of a scene of lofty passion. The latter was able to play the scene by the sheer physical resources of his technique, the former was compelled to call in the adventitious assistance of his own emotion. Obviously Talma was the greater actor.

Some photographers are prone, when working with a model, to waste a great deal of time and energy in getting the model "worked up" to the emotion they have to represent. The time is wasted because *the model's carefully cultivated emotion is a literal fact and not a pantomimic symbol.* The literal facts of the physical manifestations of actual emotion are, as I have pointed out, without pictorial value or meaning, and are subject to the wildest misinterpretation. In synthesizing an actual emotion, the photographer and the model may have an interesting or harrowing experience, but to the ultimate consumer—the man who looks at the picture—the model's emotion seems nothing but physical discomfort which is betrayed by an unpleasant grimace. Pictorially, the model's personal emotion counts for nothing; what the ultimate consumer sees in the picture counts for everything.

I have never secured anything but empty gestures and foolish grimaces when I have encouraged the model to actually feel the emotion of the scene. On the other hand, I have obtained an impression of lofty tragedy when the model's only emotion was annoyance at being kept past his lunch time. Much less than on the stage is there any justification for emotion on the part of the model: the picture is static, and there is no question of creating a *continuity* or *sustaining* a mood. At the very most, it may be permissible, early in the sitting, to allow the model one brief experimental flash of real emotion. Sometimes one is able to derive a suggestion from such a flash, pictorially useless in itself but capable of being *moulded* into a gesture or attitude which has expressive quality as pantomime.

The Limits of Expression.

Realism thus sets a limit to expression by the model. The pantomimic symbol is shattered by the intrusion of the real and the literal into the representation.

This fact is especially apparent in the handling of dramatic pictorial subjects. Drama may appear in a picture in either of two ways, explicitly or implicitly. When the drama is explicit, we have a more or less literal representation of a *scene*, a pictorial anecdote or "story-telling picture". Outstanding examples of this type are furnished by Hogarth in his "Rake's Progress" and "Marriage a la Mode". Instances of the successful use of this sort of drama in pictorial photography are exceedingly rare, though unsuccessful attempts crowd every amateur competition with reckless gestures and meaningless grimaces. These unsuccessful attempts are, in a word, pictures of drama, not dramatic pictures.

Drama of the second type, the implied, deals not with overt actions and confrontation of opponents, but with suggestions, masked emotions, power held in restraint, moments heavy with potentiality and reminders of storms just past. Thus there is definite drama in character portrayal; for character is the cumulative result of accomplished struggles. It is this dramatic perspective that distinguishes great portraits, such as da Vinci's drawing of himself as an old man or Titian's portrait of Sixtus X, from such brilliant but superficial likenesses as those of Sargent.

Obviously the second type of drama is better fitted to pictorial presentation, as there is less likelihood of the pantomimic symbol being damaged by the intrusion of literal emotion and action.

In addition to emotion, drama frequently involves *action*. The use to which action may be put in a dramatic picture must be limited by the quality of the pantomimic symbol. Action must be suggested only, not literally shown. The literal depiction of action belongs to the field of the candid-cameramen and the sports photographers who so skillfully show us the runner suspended half-way over his hurdle, the sprinter breaking the tape, and the political speaker with his mouth open and a word half-uttered. The action shown in dramatic pictures of the explicit type is generally of this sort. We frequently see it in "stills" outside motion picture theatres.

A further problem is involved when effort is made to show literal action in a dramatic picture. A dramatic moment, if more than one character is involved, consists not only of action but of *reaction*. To present action alone gives a sense of incompleteness, like a snapshot of a person walking, with one foot eternally suspended in mid-air. To simultaneously present action and reaction in the same picture (as is often done in movie "stills") produces a sense of incongruity (because reaction *follows* action) and results often in a division of interest. As seen on the screen there would be no incongruity or division of interest in the motion picture from which the above-mentioned stills were taken; for the time element would there be made evident, with reaction following action. This confusing and incongruous simultanous presentation of action and reaction in the same picture is a frequent fault of pictorial representations of explicit drama.

Action in a dramatic picture, then, is generally best presented in terms of symbol and suggestion. A phase of any given action may be found which will give the full sense of the action with the smallest amount of literal representation. Much power may be found in the suggestion that there is momentary cessation of action, that action is just about to begin, or has just been completed. In this manner a

Figure 185

"The Spanish Main"

picture outwardly passive and restrained may be intensely dramatic through the implication of the *possibilities of action*.

Compare in this respect, *The Spanish Main* (Figure 185) with *Hypatia* (Figure 186).

The Spanish Main is a thorough-going example of the picture of explicit drama. It is just the sort of moment and just the sort of interpretation that one sees in movie stills. It is, to repeat the distinction made above, a picture of drama rather than a dramatic picture. The emotion is violent and thoroughly literal in its representation. There is little or no hint of any pantomimic quality. The violent contortions of the models stir in the beholder only a mild and condescending sort of interest. The action is of the frozen type that the candid camera secures. There is division of interest because action and reaction are presented simultaneously.

"Death of Hypatia"   *William Mortensen*

Figure 186

It is interesting to note that, in making this picture, the models were encouraged to feel the utmost of genuine personal emotion. So they worked themselves up into a perfect lather of maniacal blood-lust and frenzied terror respectively, with the present obviously feeble result.

In *Hypatia,* involving likewise the composition of two figures, there is the slightest of *literal* manifestation of either emotion or action. Yet the moment is felt to be heavy with the direst of possibilities. In making this picture, needless to say, there was no effort at stirring up the models to emotional manifestations: all effort was bent to arranging the plastic and pantomimic elements.

Representation of Movement.

Literal representation of action should be avoided, as we have seen, and should be suggested as just beginning or just completed. A somewhat different problem is involved in the representation of *movement.* Some kinds of movement may be legitimately suggested in a picture. These are the types of movement that characteristically pertain to the person or thing represented. Thus, it is characteristic of marching soldiers that they *march,* of a dancer that she *dances,* and of the ocean, that its waves continue to beat upon the shore. Such movement is generally rhythmic and cyclic, repeating the same pattern with little variation. In pictorial representation of movement of this kind, the problem is to find the particular moment in the cycle that will best give the sense of the movement and its continued flow. This moment is generally found at the culminating point of the cycle; the climactic point at which there is a hint of momentary cessation of movement. Thus a wave is best represented when it hangs with over-curved crest just an instant before it dissolves in foam and confusion. Marching soldiers are best represented with the feet at the top of their swing, and the best sense of the dancer's movement is given by the height of her gesture.

Expressive Qualities of Male and Female Bodies.

The expressive quality of the male body differs greatly from that of the female body. Incongruity, especially in the case of nudes, results from the artist's failure to take this difference into account. Without intending such an effect, he may find that his male figures are epicene, or his female figures masculine in suggestion.

The basic expressive quality of the female figure is that of *being admired*. It is definitely passive in its suggestion. Violent activity in a nude female figure is therefore usually felt as incongruous. Unless there is logical basis for the absence of clothes—as in Gerome's *Phryne*—drama or powerful emotion should not be combined with the representation of the female nude. This unhappy combination is one of the things that is wrong with pictures of a certain well-known type—nude female figures being represented in the throes of violent and false emotion, bearing such titles as "Remorse", "Exaltation", etc.

The male figure, on the other hand, connotes and expresses *activity*. The best expositions of the masculine nude have been those that have shown it in fight and combat, as in the metopes of the Parthenon, the Laocoon group, etc. Even such an outwardly passive figure as Rodin's *Thinker* expresses a terrific inward struggle that is so primitive that it actually rises to the muscular level. Such thinking as Professor Einstein's cerebration of the General Theory of Relativity could not, however, be expressed in plastic terms.

Expressive Use of "Errors".

In Chapter Six in Part One I mentioned that there were circumstances under which certain of the plastic errors of posing might be intentionally introduced into a picture. The sole justification for their introduction is *greater expressiveness*. The "errors" are so called because, by their inclusion in a pose, they give a false or perverted impression of the structure of the human body. Generally speaking, the human structure should be accepted as one of the premises of pictorial expression. Occasionally, however, one has to deal with an idea that is best expressed by breaking rather than preserving this structure.

For example, in *Steel Stocks Advance* (Figure 187) the idea is one that passes beyond conventional plastic expression. The "broken wrist" was deliberately and intentionally introduced because it seemed to express most clearly and concisely the pathos of the broken body and the rigidity of death.

In *Girl of the Highlands* (Figure 188) the right angled elbow was permitted to remain because, by its masculine connotation, it gave an additional emphasis to the model's expression of strength and independence.

The foreshortened torse in *The Priestess* (Figure 189) has expressive value. The fact that the body leans away from the observer carries out the impression of remoteness and inaccessible majesty.

"Girl of the Highlands" *William Mortensen*

Figure 188

Had the body been erect or inclined toward the observer, the priestess would have seemed to condescend and to listen graciously.

Here are a few other possible expressive uses of errors. Old age and extreme decrepitude naturally call for the use of a *slumped scapula* and of a *collapsed abdomen*. A *flat foot in profile* might be an appropriate part of a pose of a peasant type, expressing stability and close contact with the soil. The ugly and angular posture of the *hand above the ilium* may be useful in indicating vulgar belligerency.

Before proceeding to the rather bold step of including errors for their expressive value, the photographer should ask himself two questions:

1. Is the plastic or the expressive purpose the primary one in this subject?
2. Is the introduction of the error the best possible method of expression?

With plastic subjects, such as nudes, the expressive elements must be of the greatest delicacy. In such subjects the discordant emphasis of errors would be utterly incongruous—like a Stravinsky dissonance in the middle of a Hayden minuet.

Often the idea that one seeks may be expressed just as well by keeping within the limits of bodily structure. In such a case, it is best to keep within these limits instead of proceeding to the extremity of deliberately introducing errors.

This section provides no alibi for the careless and needless inclusion of errors. Errors must be included only with careful intent and realization of their significance. There is never any excuse for introducing several errors at once. The very expressive value of an error depends upon its isolation.

Relation of Figure and Background.

A special problem of the expressive qualities of the model is involved in *the use of figures in landscape.*

Landscape and the human figure are two diverse and different

"The Priestess"   *William Mortensen*

Figure 189

elements. Landscape is largely a matter of *mood*, and in the creation of this mood *lighting effects* are all-important. The human figure, on the other hand, carries formal and personal implications. In the representation of the figure, lighting is secondary and generally exists merely for the sake of visibility.*

Because of their diverse nature, figure and landscape cannot function equally in the same picture. One or the other must dominate. And, in any given picture, the artist must be very clear in his own mind, and must make it very clear to the observer, *which* of the two elements is intended to play the principal role.

Thus there are two different and distinct uses of figures in landscapes, and two different ways of combining figures and backgrounds. These are:

    1. Figure dominant, landscape incidental.

    2. Landscape dominant, figure incidental.

The first type of combination is well represented in the work of Alexander Keighley. In his pictures the landscape is simply a gorgeous but subordinate "back drop" in front of which is played the drama of his figures.

Leonard Misonne's pictures represent, as a rule, the second type of combination. He uses his subordinate human figures merely as fingers, as it were, that point the way into the picture. And, having thus coaxed the attention into the picture, these figures gracefully yield it up to the dominant landscape interest.

Any picture in which there is anything like equal interest in figure and landscape is, inevitably, a bad picture. One element or the other must unmistakably dominate.

There are numerous pictorial methods by which the artist may emphasize or subordinate, if he chooses, the figures in a landscape. Here are some of the more important methods:

    1. *Lighting.* Strong light on figure emphasizes it. Figure in shadow is subordinate.

    2. *Position.* Figure near center of picture is more emphatic than near edge.

---

*For discussion of the pictorial function of light see Pictorial Lighting, Chapter Two.

Figure 190

3. *Size.* Large figure dominates, small figure is subordinate.
4. *Tone.* A costume of tone contrary to the background stresses the figure, a costume of similar tone subordinates it. Thus a dark costume is emphatic against a light background, and subordinate against a dark one.
5. *Contrast.* If figure contains in itself an extreme range of contrast, it is emphatic. If contrast is slight, figure is subordinated.
6. *Detail.* Inclusion of detail in figure emphasizes it. Lack of detail subordinates it.
7. *Face.* Figure facing observer is emphatic. Figure turned away is subordinate.

Figure 191

8. *Direction of movement.* Movement toward observer emphasizes figure. Movement away from the observer (into the picture) subordinates it. (Note that in Misonne's pictures the figures that travel his rutted roads are usually moving away from you.)

9. *Gesture.* A gesture by the figure commands attention. A quiescent figure is subordinate.

Figure 190 and Figure 191 show the two methods of combining figure and background. In Figure 190 the figure is subordinated by being kept in the *shadow,* by its *inferior position,* by its relatively *small size,* by the *dark tone* of its costume, by its *lack of contrast,* by the complete *lack of detail,* and by the fact that it *faces away* from the observer. At the same time, the architectural background is emphasized by the *lighting, large size, greater contrast,* and *more detail.*

In Figure 191 the figure is dominant. It is emphasized by receiving the principal *illumination,* by its *conspicuous position,* by its relatively *large size,* by its *large range of contrast,* by the *detail* which it includes, and by the fact that the *face* is shown. The background is, on the other hand, subordinated by being kept in the *shadow,* which in turn *reduces the contrast and the amount of detail.*

PART THREE

Problems of Direction

CHAPTER ONE

The General Aims of Direction

The two preceding sections of this book have dealt with the two phases—physical and expressive—of the model's contribution to the picture. We now come more specifically to the artist's part in the project. The model may have the requisite physical characteristics and ample expressive ability, but, unless the artist is able to make use of these things by *securing the desired response* from the model, all the model's qualifications and abilities count for nothing.

Direction is the method by which the artist secures such response from the model as will lead to the production of a picture.

Part of direction is concerned with the practical problems of securing the proper physical basis and the expressive qualities that we discussed in the two preceding sections. But there is also the equally important *personal* problem of the relationship between artist and model. The practical problems cannot be properly dealt with until the personal one is understood. This matter of personal relationship is so important because it determines the model's *mental attitude* toward the sitting and the projected picture. A hostile, apprehensive or indifferent model is scarcely better than no model at all. Unless there is this proper mental attitude on the part of the model, the most workmanlike arranging of the latter's limbs, the most skillful evoking of his or her emotions, will avail little towards securing a picture. Thus *all* personal relationship of artist and model may become concerned in direction.

There are, therefore, *three principal aims* in the direction of a model:

1. To secure proper mental attitude.
2. To secure proper physical response.
3. To secure proper emotional expression.

Three Bad Model Reactions.

In securing a useful and cooperative attitude toward the business of making a picture there are three especially bad reactions of the model that must at all costs be avoided. They are all negative and destructive, and the presence of any one of them is sufficient to wreck the prospects of any sitting. These are the three:

1. Resentment.
2. Boredom.
3. Distraction.

These three reactions constitute an obstacle that the best of photographers with the best of pictorial material and all the time in the world cannot surmount. If the model is resentful, bored or inattentive, the unhappy fact always grins through in the finished picture.

How shall these reactions be avoided? Possibly the best way to avoid arousing resentment in the model is to understand its causes.

Causes of Resentment.

As the first of these causes we may mention a *faulty attitude on the part of the artist* himself. This wrong attitude may take any one of four different forms, but it is due in all cases to a feeling of inferiority on the part of the artist. These four wrong attitudes, all

191

motivated by inferiority, are:

1. Cheap flippancy. The artist tries to wisecrack his way out of his embarrassment. This results in reducing the picture to a secondary issue, with an inevitable indifferent and half-way sort of result. The model naturally resents this cheap approach.

2. Timid vacillation. The artist is too scared to make any definite and coherent suggestion. The model either despises him for his timorousness or else thoroughly resents him because she suspects his timidity conceals an ulterior motive.

3. Tyranny. The artist attempts to brazen out his insufficient knowledge and uncertainty by a hard-boiled belligerent attitude which implies that the model is a mere beast of burden.

4. Egotism. Sometimes the inferiority complex asserts itself in the form of brassy self-assertion. The artist devotes the sitting to impressing the model and bragging about the salons he has crashed.

A frequent cause of resentment is *apparent lack of appreciation* on the part of the artist. When the model is giving his or her best effort to the making of the picture and is getting hot, tired and uncomfortable, the artist, unless he is careful, is apt to get so absorbed in his own problem that he takes the model's contribution for granted. A word of flattery goes a long way toward securing a good reaction from the model. As a matter of fact, the flattery may be laid on with quite a lavish hand. It is a curious psychological quirk that a model when posing will eagerly soak up fulsome praise that would be laughed off under any other circumstances as outrageous flattery.

Men are resentful of too much ceremony. They have come to have their picture taken or to be in a picture, and, while they are willing to work hard, they want to arrive at the main problem with as little fussing around as possible.

With women, a particular cause of resentment is *jealousy*. If two or more women are included in a picture, or if one woman looks on while another models, the problem of jealously is apt to arise. Posing provides especially rich ground for feminine jealousy because rival exhibitionisms are brought into competition for favorable notice.

"*The White Hibiscus*"   *William Mortensen*

When several women appear in one picture, it is wise and diplomatic to avoid featuring one of them to the exclusion of the others. Make an appearance at least of featuring each of them in turn.* The other source of jealousy is dealt with by avoiding, so far as possible, the presence of female spectators while another woman is working as model.** In fact, it is wisest not to clutter up a sitting with any spectators of any sex.

Resentment may easily develop, especially with a new or inexperienced model, if the artist is obscure or vague in his instructions. The artist may be clear in his own mind as to what he wants, but he must, for the model's benefit, take particular pains to put his ideas into clear, simple and consistent terms. Unless he is careful on this point, the model will speedily become annoyed at being unjustly placed in a stupid light. Some specific suggestions for clarifying directions and instructions to models will be given a little later in this chapter.

A thoughtless artist may arouse resentment by imposing too much on a willing model. Most models *are* willing, but enough's enough. A stage is reached when weariness is too great to be borne: a rest period should then be called, or the sitting terminated. No matter how good a sport the model may be, the artist should know when to draw the line in asking the performance of an act that is definitely dangerous, unpleasant or painful. The artist should never demand anything of a model that he is not willing to do himself.***

Summing up, the general cause of resentment may be described as *lack of tact and consideration.* This formula is broad enough to include the specific causes we have described and any others that may arise. To realize the best possible results from models, the artist must be a subtle diplomat as well as a person of human sympathy, and be capable of simple kindness as well as Machiavellian stratagems.

*This problem is further discussed in connection with the use of groups in pictures, Chapter Three, Part Three.

**The presence of a maid, of different race and social status, is quite permissible. There is not, under these circumstances, any element of competition involved.

***It is sometimes best in such questionable cases for the artist to take over the model's task. The author played the uncomfortable leading role in The Vampire. (Monsters & Madonnas, 1936.)

To Avoid Boredom.

Resentment has at least the advantage of being an active and wide-awake reaction, no matter how unfortunate and destructive it may be otherwise. Boredom, on the other hand, is simply slow death. The model's original interest in the project will, if it finds nothing to sustain itself, wither and fade away. *The artist must learn to plan and conduct the sitting in such a manner as to keep the model's interest not only alive but growing.*

Realization of this general fact is the best preventive of boredom; but a few more specific suggestions may be made.

In the first place, the artist should know, and should show that he knows, what he is doing. Or, if he is uncertain, he should never let the model suspect the fact. At the first sign of uncertainty, vagueness or fumbling, the model loses interest. One of the advantages of such preliminary preparations as plans and sketches is that they enable the artist to swing immediately into a *definite* problem. Avoid in any case too much deliberation and obvious experimentation at the beginning of the sitting. Give the model's interest something *concrete* to cope with at the outset: later, when his or her interest is *established*, the model will gladly follow you into all sorts of experimentation.

A necessary factor in arousing and maintaining the model's interest is, of course, a corresponding interest on the part of the artist. If the artist appears to be uninterested and blase about the sitting, it is not to be expected that the model will arise to the occasion. The artist need not bubble or gush, but he should show interest in what he is doing. If he is not capable of genuine enthusiasm about the pic-torial project, there is no excuse for his undertaking it, and he is merely wasting the model's time and his own.

It is to the advantage of both the artist and the model to conduct the sitting at a quite *rapid tempo*. A rapid tempo makes the artist give his attention to the picture that he is making and to the model that is before him, and prevents him from becoming involved in the mechanical complications of his camera. The same rapid tempo

195

keeps the model on the alert, and assures him that something is going on. To keep up the impression of speed, the artist should take—or pretend to take—numerous shots of all stages of the sitting. Film is the cheapest ingredient that goes into a sitting, and it is poor economy to be sparing of exposures. If a pose is quite hopeless and film is running low, maintain the impression of speed by going through all the motions of taking numerous exposures— with the black slide left in place. A bit of elementary sleight-of-hand will convey the impression that several pictures have been taken—and thus save the model's feelings. *Never let the model down.*

A natural obstacle to the model's continued interest lies in the inherently static quality of the act of posing. It is difficult for a model to maintain the impression that something is happening when he has not moved for five minutes himself, when his neck is getting stiff, and his nose itches, and his foot is asleep. To keep up the feeling of action and "something doing" the artist should direct the model to break the pose occasionally and to resume it after a few second's rest. This practice reacts to the advantage of the pose also, for a pose that is held too long becomes wooden and tense, despite the best effort of model and artist. When the pose is broken and picked up again, it will be found to have all the good plastic qualities that it formerly had, plus a new vitality and spontaneity.

A well-directed sitting will have something of the quality of a good plan—a constant building and development of tension and excitement. The interest of model and artist both should be carried along on this current of common enthusiasm. To make the sitting *move* in this way, the artist must *work*, must give of himself. An artist who finishes a sitting with his respiration, pulse and the part of his hair unaltered, has probably obtained very poor results.

Too great intimacy and familiarity between model and artist may prove a source of boredom. Because of too frequent repetition, the sitting becomes for both a matter of uneventful routine. Routine sittings rarely produce anything but routine results. There should be a definite psychological barrier separating the functions of artist and model, the artist controlling and the model subservient. It is to the advantage of both to preserve the sense of this barrier. So when matters reach a stage when the model is able to foresee resignedly every suggestion of the artist, and when the artist finds himself more interested in the model than in the picture—it is time to call quits for awhile. Possibly the stimulus of a new and exciting pictorial subject may serve to arouse a fresh and impersonal interest in both. If not, artist and model should suspend operations for a month or so. At the end of this mutual vacation, they will be able to return to work with renewed interest and their proper relationship re-established.

The psychological barrier between model and artist is a very important one and quite necessary to their proper functioning in making a picture. Model and artist both should strive to maintain this barrier and be on their guard to prevent the destructive element of intimacy from creeping into their relationship.

One other kind of boredom should be mentioned—*constitutional boredom*. Once in awhile one meets a model that is bored before the sitting, is gently bored throughout the sitting, and is bored at the end of the sitting—in fact, one can only surmise that she was born bored. Neither direction nor dynamite can prevail against this mild and bovine ennui. A model of this sort is very limited in her usefulness. Only by happy and improbable accident can she be of value in dramatic subjects. If her figure is good enough to compensate for the trouble, she may prove of use in plastic compositions of a completely inert and placid type.

Sources of Distraction.

The third type of bad reaction that prevents the model from attaining a proper mental attitude toward the sitting and its problems is *distraction*. Many things may serve to distract a model and prevent him or her from concentrating on the issue at hand, but the principal sources of distraction may be summed up under four headings:

In the first place, the distraction or interruption may arise from within the model herself. (It is generally female models that offend in this manner.) Certain models, sometimes because of nervousness, sometimes from sheer nitwittedness, are inclined to make a joke of the whole matter, and to punctuate the sitting with giggles, titters and gales of laughter. Such a model must be dealt with sternly. If she does not prove amenable to discipline, she should be forthwith dropped from future consideration as a model. Such a person may be the life of the party—when she is at a party; but in a studio she is a demoralizing and disruptive influence.

Another possible source of distraction is an artist with an untimely sense of humor. A gift for repartee is a valuable possession, but the artist who parades it at unsuitable moments is defeating his own end. The success of certain sorts of pictorial material depends upon creating and sustaining, even during the sitting, a definite mood and illusion. This is particularly true of costume pictures with a suggestion of "period". This illusion is a very delicate structure into which a modern wisecrack crashes, like a baseball into a piece of Venetian glass. The artist gets his response: the model laughs—dutifully, hysterically, or resentfully, as the case may be; but the mood is irretrievably shattered.

A third source of distraction arises from *extraneous personalities* at the sitting. A mob of chattering friends and relatives should of course never be tolerated. The picture is primarily the problem of the artist and the model. The presence of other persons, even though silent and well-behaved, may prove a distracting influence. Models vary in their reaction to spectators. Some are not bothered, a few are actually stimulated by the presence of a "gallery". Still others, however, are rendered extremely uncomfortable and self-conscious by the intrusion of extraneous personalities. The chattering relatives should be eliminated with as little delay and ceremony as possible. The best practice is to allow *no* spectators at a sitting unless it is absolutely certain that they will not prove a source of distraction.

Finally, there is distraction which *arises from mechanical complications*. Various manifestations of the Machine and its brood of

small monsters are always conspiring to interrupt the sitting. Films must be changed, cameras focused, diaphragm settings adjusted, lights juggled and exposures made. The inexperienced photographer, if he allows himself to become involved in these things, will work himself into a perspiring frenzy over them, and his model into a state of nervous apprehension. Instead, the photographer should always strive to reduce these operations to a mere ritual which involves the fingers but not the mind, and which is carried off with a Murad-inspired nonchalance. Nothing should be allowed to interrupt the smooth flow of the sitting.

The lighting units are mechanical elements that are particularly liable to worry a model. They dazzle one, stare one down, flood one's deformities, physical and moral, with their harsh radiance—and never seem to be correctly adjusted. These characteristics of lighting units are especially apparent when the units are numerous, huge, inordinately bright, and weirdly shaped. But even a single small unit may become very upsetting to the model if the artist juggles it about distractedly. Avoid shifting the units suddenly and abruptly. Instead, work by a series of small adjustments. There are actual dangers involved in the handling of lights: if a recklessly plunging photographer trips over a light cord, a nude model may receive serious and disfiguring burns from the overturned light unit.* Have consideration for your model's eyes. Prolonged exposure of their eyes to strong light causes some people great distress. Permit your models to close their eyes, if they wish, between exposures and during changes in set-up. If it is necessary to bring a unit very close to the model's face, the light should not be left burning continuously.

Factors in Securing Proper Physical Response.

I have suggested that there are three principal aims in the direction of a model:

1. To secure proper mental attitude.
2. To secure proper physical response.
3. To secure proper emotional expression.

We have considered the first aim in terms of obstacles that prevent its attainment. We come now to the consideration of factors that assist in attaining the second aim—proper physical response.

The first factor, and a very important one, is *clear* direction. In other words, the model must be made to know what you are talking about. Clear direction is *not* highfalutin language nor vague and misty appeals to the imagination, ending with a hopeful suggestion to the model that they do *something* along that line. On the contrary, *good direction is definite, concrete, and concise.* It says, in effect, "The idea of the picture is thus and so. You will wear this and make up thus. We will begin with you standing in this manner. Turn your head to the right. Raise your right shoulder. Depress your left elbow. . . ." And so on.

---

*This is one of the risks against which the photographer should protect himself by some form of liability insurance. (See Appendix B.)

An essential part of clear direction is a mutually accepted *vocabulary of commands*. To accomplish anything, even with the simplest sort of physical adjustments, model and artist must have a background of common experience and understanding. The vocabulary supplies the first step toward this common background. To avoid long hours of fruitless haggling, it is immediately necessary that artist and model establish between themselves a concise and convenient vocabulary of commands whereby the artist directs the model in arriving at a desired pose. This vocabulary should be brief and definite, and learning to work by it should be the first task of a new model. Only as a last resort, which concedes either the artist's inarticulateness or the model's stupidity, should it prove necessary for the artist to make a bodily adjustment by touching the model. Of course, the arranging of details of costume and the placing of locks of hair come under a different category: in these cases it is frequently desirable for the artist to make the adjustment himself.

Every artist will find it best to create his own vocabulary of commands, but a few suggestions may be made. In regard to Right and Left, let the artist accept the convention of the stage director, and command "Right" or "Left" in terms of the *model's* right or left. Distinguish immediately between "tipping the head" and "turning the head". (For example, the head in Figure 34 is *tipped* to her left, that in Figure 39 is *turned* to her right.)

A small and obvious point of direction, yet one that is frequently forgotten, is the need of warning the model before each exposure with some such phrase as "Hold it!" or "Still!" Failure to do this will result in many losses through movement. Lack of warning is also liable to arouse resentment in a model. An inexperienced model will need to be cautioned also against moving between the initial and concluding clicks of a time exposure.

A second factor in securing proper physical response is the training of the model. A new model, no matter how willing, is more difficult to secure accurate physical response from, owing to his or her ignorance of the conventions and limitations of the act of posing.

A well-trained model, for example, will move *slowly* in answer to a command. Too prompt or abrupt a response may shatter the whole pose. Rather than leaping instantly into the new position, the model should strive to move slowly *towards* it. The artist may then stop the movement when the desired degree of alteration is reached.

In the later stages of refining a pose it is essential that the model acquire the trick of adjusting the position of one part of the body without changing the conformation of the rest. The model should be able, for example, to adjust the arrangement of a hand without moving the arm. Or to lean forward or back without changing the angle of head and shoulders. Or to move the head slowly and delicately without moving the shoulders.

With experience, an intelligent model will come to appreciate the limitations of the camera, and will adjust his or her movements to conform to them. Such a model will instinctively come to plan poses in camera terms—that is, in terms of a plane at right angles to the axis of the lens, avoiding all gestures or actions extending toward or away from the camera. It is sometimes helpful to new models to suggest that they imagine themselves attached to a wall on which they form bas-relief patterns.

Another factor in securing proper physical response from a model is the application of universal artistic practice to the photographer's procedure in building up a pose. An essential part of this practice is the principle of establishing large masses before bothering with details. Amateurs working with models for the first time are very apt to violate this principle. To start the sitting by fussing with the position of the hands, with the precise angle of the chin, or with a lesser detail of costume, can lead only to confusion.

In building up the physical basis of a pose it is best to work along the following systematic lines:

1. As a painter lays in the main masses of his picture with charcoal, *rough in the main idea* of your pose. This "main idea" may consist of a pencil sketch, or of a hazily visualized mental

pattern, or of little more than an emotional reaction. But whatever it is, place the main masses of your model's body to conform roughly to this idea.

2. When the pose is roughed in, stand off and examine it impersonally. Numerous obvious and major errors will become apparent. Proceed then to *eliminate the major errors.*

3. You have now the corrected general basis of the pose. Proceed next to *adjust details,* working with progressively smaller items of pose, hair-dress and costume.

4. Finally, examine the set-up once more. Wherever possible, *eliminate the minor errors* that become evident. It is necessary to proceed with caution in the elimination of minor errors, for one may find that he has also eliminated the spontaneity and vitality of the pose. It is also possible, as I pointed out in Part Two, that some of the effectiveness of the pose may be due to the expressive use of a plastic error.

For the sake of maintaining the interest of the model, it will be necessary to begin shooting early in the procedure. Even though, to the artist's eye, the pose is far from perfect, it should be recorded. The act of taking exposures builds up the impression of something doing, something accomplished, and stimulates the model to further effort. This practice is occasionally profitable in other ways also; for sometimes an unsuspected picture will reveal itself in a proof of an early crude stage of a pose.

Factors in Securing Emotional Expression.

The third aim of direction, as I have outlined at the beginning of this chapter, is the securing of proper *emotional expression.*

In Part One we emphasized the necessity of a clearly established plastic basis for thought or emotion. As this physical basis is the *sine qua non* of any sort of pictorial representation, we have dealt with it first.

In actual practice, the relating of thought and emotion to the plastic form is not so simple. Despite the primary importance of the plastic basis, emotion and thought are in no wise to be regarded as mere veneers that are pasted on over the plastic foundation. From the *artist's* point of view, thought and emotion frequently guide the whole process, setting the key for the pose, and providing an element of unification. But in dealing with the model the problem is different. Too early introduction of emotional or expressive issues needlessly complicates things, and distracts one from the immediate physical problem of posing the body. Furthermore, there are certain expressive actions that cannot be adequately suggested by mere synthetic physical adjustments.

There are two methods by which thought and action may be related to the plastic basis. The choice of method depends upon the type of pictorial material.

1. For a passive, quiescent sort of composition such as *Give Us This Day* (Figure 192), the whole simple plastic basis may be built up without suggesting any emotion to the models. When the basis is well in hand, the emotion may then be suggested, completing and unifying the picture.

2. In a picture involving an active, violent composition, the first method is not feasible. It is necessary in such a case to suggest the emotion or thought to the model at the outset. The model, if at all competent, can create from this suggestion the beginning of the plastic basis of the picture. It will probably be crude and faulty, but the artist will be able to correct and refine upon it along the lines of the procedure just discussed. During this period of correction and refinement, the thought or emotion is forgotten, and the problem becomes again a purely plastic one.

"Give Us This Day"   *William Mortensen*

Figure 192

205

CHAPTER TWO

The Three Types of Models

Models (being but human) differ widely in personality, intelligence, sensitivity and initiative. The proper handling of each model to secure the fullest and most expressive results is, for the experienced artist, a new and *individual* problem. However, it is possible, without losing sight of the individual aspects of the problem, to classify models in three general categories. By understanding and learning to recognize these categories and by the practice of "pigeon-holing" all models on this basis one may much simplify the multifarious problems of directions.

These three classes of models represent (as I have outlined in the Introduction) three different conditions of working that may characterize the association of artist with model. To reiterate, these conditions are:

1. The artist is dominant.
2. The model is dominant.
3. There is cooperation between the two.

It is true that some accomplished models are able to adapt themselves to any of these three conditions. Nevertheless, these conditions represent *three different and distinct types* of models, of widely different background and qualifications. It is essential that one learn to discriminate between these types, as each is adapted to a different sort of picture and requires different handling. These three types we may for brevity's sake designate as follows:

1. The passive (or plastic) type.
2. The personal type.
3. The cooperative type.

The condition of complete dominance of the artist over the model is appropriate to pictures in which the emphasis is on purely *plastic* elements. Neither personality nor drama enter into the picture: the model is, in effect, passive clay which the potter-artist moulds to his will. Most nudes belong in this category. So also do many pictures in which large groups are used. Such pictures, particularly if they are being evolved from a preconceived sketch, are concerned with large problems of composition rather than individual expressiveness.

For the passive type the principal qualification is the physical one. If nudes are in view, of course the figure must be good and the carriage graceful. No great intelligence is demanded of this type nor any particular dramatic power, but the model must possess the ability to subordinate himself or herself to the artist's direction. Excessive exuberance or flightiness is a definite handicap. If the model is intelligent and has dramatic ability, there is possibility that he or she may be developed up to the point of doing pictures of the cooperative type. Indeed, extensive work under the passive condition is the best training and preparation for a model of the latter type.

When the model is dominant, we have the working condition that results in vivid portraiture. The *personality* of the sitter shines forth, unadorned by any comment or obvious arrangement by the artist. The acceptance of this working condition assumes that the model possesses a photographically effective personality. This condition is, naturally, the appropriate one for photographing professional actors. Ideally, it is appropriate for all portraiture; but, unhappily, not all who come to sit for pictures have personalities that are immediately effective in the photographic medium. In such cases the photographer is obliged to exert his directorial prerogative and endeavor to create a pseudo-personality that will be acceptable to friends and relatives.*

Models of the personal type are readily identified by their immediately arresting and vital quality. Portraiture of notables of stage and screen and public life deals, in effect, with models of this type. The persons themselves, what they are, how they express themselves, these matters are the central interest, not how the artist expresses himself through them. The artist's task with such a model is primarily one of recording vivid and significant moments. He must practice severe self-abnegation, rigidly excluding his own personality from the problem. The model must feel no slightest sense of restraint, but must be encouraged to take the lead, to be himself utterly, to express himself fully. Meanwhile, the artist exercises, as unobtrusively as possible, some control in preventing unpleasant errors in arrangement.

The condition of *cooperation*, the third possible relationship between artist and model, must exist for the production of pictures in which an *idea* is involved. When interpretation into pictorial terms of a dramatic theme or characterization is sought for, it may be obtained only by a sympathetic collaboration of artist and model. This collaboration need not be obvious or physical. There is no need for extensive and long-winded consultation. But sympathy there must be, a sense of *rapport*, and an identity of purpose. Such collaboration is from the very nature of things rare, but from it spring the finest accomplishments in pictorial art.

Usually a model is not equipped to qualify for this condition of working until he or she has had considerable experience in working before the camera in problems of the passive type. Under these circumstances an occasional model will reveal, by ready intelligence and an aptitude for dramatic expression, a fitness for coping with more significant pictorial problems. Such a one, by training, may evolve into what is the highest type of model, one that is capable of genuinely collaborating with the artist. Only by the use of a model of this

*The uses of the personal type is considered in these pages only in relation to the "pictorial portrait." The problems of commercial portraiture, which are of course embraced under this condition of working, would lead us too far afield. These problems—and they are many—must await later treatment.

"Myrdith
William Mortensen

sort is it possible to escape from the shortcomings of the other two types—the emotional lack of the first and the topical character of the second—and to achieve pictorial work that is solid in substance and authentic in emotion, with perfect balance between control and expression. The combination of apparent spontaneity with fine composition is the rarest of pictorial qualities, and may be attained only by patient cooperative effort of model and artist. Photography is probably the only medium that permits of such complete cooperation.

For a model of this type a native dramatic ability is generally more useful than a background of professional or stage experience. There is apt to be a certain over-facility and smugness about the work of professionals. They are inclined to utilize stock effects from their repertory instead of the sincerely felt emotions that the untrained actor strives for. The eye may be impressed by the slickness of the professional's work, but the less impressionable camera detects and reveals any note of insincerity.

The next three chapters will be concerned with the various special problems involved in directing these three types of models.

CHAPTER THREE

The Plastic Model.

The condition of working in which the artist is dominant in all stages of the sitting finds its realization in the plastic model. The term "plastic" not only expresses the physical function of this sort of model—the malleable material which the artist shapes as he wishes —but also well describes the characteristic mentality of this type. A self-assertive nature and an active brain are definitely antipathetic to the best work of the plastic category. Rather, a gentle and amenable disposition should be sought. Ideally, a mind that is a *tabula rasa*, open to all impressions and free from all predispositions, is the proper mentality for a model of the plastic type.

The nude and the group picture are the two most important and characteristic uses of the purely plastic model. In a model that is to be used in a nude picture the only significant qualifications are physical ones. Both the self-assertion of the personality model and the dramatic expression of the cooperative model are out of place in a nude. It is perhaps regrettable, but neither intelligence nor virtue seems to be very effective pictorially. The Dumb Doras are frequently useful in pictures of the plastic type, while the knock-kneed Hypatias fail miserably. And a street walker may reveal (pictorially) greater spirituality than the president of the W. C. T. U.

Photographers sometimes sneer at the Dumb Dora type of model. "Tillie is absolutely hopeless", they will assert. "She is completely dead pan. I can get no expression out of her at all." This assertion shows too much readiness to pass on the blame. It may be freely granted that Tillie is a mental light weight. The trouble, however, lies not in her "dead pan", but in the dead brain of the photographer. No model is too dumb, but some artists are too stupid to realize the possibilities of what is given them. A resourceful artist could find effective material among the residents of a Home for Half-Wits.

Previous experience is of secondary importance with a plastic model—provided she has the physical qualifications. Indeed, experience may even prove disadvantageous if it upsets the model's complaisant simplicity of mind and gives her notions and prepossessions about how things should be done. Dumb and amenable is much more useful than experienced and willful. For this reason, there is little if any advantage in employing professional models. The model for a nude picture need possess only one thing—the physical qualifications.

However, these qualifications must be of the very highest. Only the finest of figures may qualify for use in nudes. Nudes are not made by merely removing the clothes from models. Nudes are, without doubt, the most difficult to do of all pictures. A photographer who attempts to follow this difficult line of work with a model that is physically inferior has hopelessly handicapped himself at the start.

Personal Relationships.

Obviously, the relationship of photographer and nude model involves delicate problems of tact and taste.

The most important general principle that governs this relationship is this: *The removal of clothes removes no barriers.* The customary relationship of artist and model is in no wise altered by the accident of nudity. The attitude of the artist toward the model should be, as always, kindly and respectful, never degrading into banal familiarity. On the other hand, all false prudery and lack of frankness should be avoided. Nor should the artist fail to pay the model

"*Study*"   *William Mortensen*

the tribute of admiration.*

The first time a model poses in the nude for a photographer is always a touchy proceeding. It calls for the utmost tact on the part of the photographer. He must realize the model's probable embarrassment and act accordingly. He should avoid any prolonged or obvious scrutiny. His manner should be matter-of-fact, impersonal and serious, but should never suggest brusqueness. By working swiftly and plunging immediately into the problem at hand the model's mind may be distracted from the strangeness of the situation. The model should be made to feel that *both she and the artist are secondary to the picture.* If photographers would exercise more care, consideration and tact, it would happen less often that a model's first session of posing in the nude is also her last.

How shall an inexperienced model be introduced to the question of posing in the nude? Probably the worst of all ways of accomplishing this is the slow disrobing method practiced by some photographers—a gradual insinuating away of the model's clothes. This "strip tease" method is open to numerous objections. In the first place, it is definitely erotic in its implications. Furthermore, it has a most unfortunate effect on the model. The gradual removal of her clothes makes her all the more keenly aware of them and her need of them. When the ultimate garment is removed, she is so thoroughly embarrassed that there is little hope of securing good pictures.

A preferable method is to remove no clothes at the model's first sitting. But take a few pictures that are quite decollette. At this point discontinue the sitting. At the second sitting the model will frequently suggest of her own accord that nude pictures be taken.**

From being very timid and shrinking at the first sitting in the nude a model is apt, unless she is restrained from it, to swing reck-

*I cannot pass over this subject without pausing to pay tribute to the late Arthur Kales for his remarkable skill in dealing with models. No one knew so truly as he how to obtain the finest response from a model, and no one ever treated his models with greater kindliness and tact. He worked with many models; but whether he was dealing with Ruth St. Denis, a bucolic beauty-contest winner, or the humblest Hollywood extra—all were treated with the identical fine consideration and impersonality. These relationships were marked with the same delicacy that characterized the unforgettable bromoil transfers of this great pictorialist.

**Further discussion of the diplomacy involved in asking a model to pose in the nude will be found in Monsters & Madonnas (Cinderella).

"Ionia"   *William Mortensen*

lessly to the other extreme. While changes in set-up are being made, she will lounge about unclothed in commonplace, casual attitudes, smoking a cigarete, or even dash to answer the telephone.

Such careless procedure on the part of the model reacts to her own disadvantage, and to the disadvantage of the artist and the picture. The plastic representation of the nude must maintain an impression of remoteness and ideality. Nothing can so utterly destroy this ideality as the sight of the nude body in familiar and commonplace attitudes engaged in familiar and commonplace activities.

Therefore, the model should wear, and the artist should see that she wears, a robe or covering of some sort when leaving or returning to her dressing room, and she should resume this garment at all pauses in the sitting. There is no issue of morality involved here; it is simply good sense that both model and artist should protect themselves from the consequences of disillusionment.

Empathy.

The aestheticians who have studied the psychological bases of art have evolved one concept that is of genuine value to the practical artist. This is the notion of "empathy" (a translation of the German term "Einfühlung").

This word is possibly alarming in appearance, but its meaning is simple, and the concept which it involves is a familiar one. The meaning is perhaps best appreciated by literally translating the German term: Einfühlung means "feeling into". This term expresses our constant human tendency to project ourselves into the object which we contemplate, and to participate, by a sort of inner mimicry, in its activity.

For example, when looking at a mountain we say, "The mountain *rises* above the plain". Looking at the plain, we say, "It *spreads* out". Looking at a church with an inordinately large tower, we say, "The tower *crushes* the church". Of course, the mountain does not actually rise, the plain does not really spread itself at all, nor is the church actually crushed. What happens is that the upward sloping lines of the mountain give us a *feeling* of rising, the horizontal lines of the plain give us a *feeling* of extension, and the bulk of the tower gives us a *feeling* of weight. These feelings we project into, and identify with, the objects that cause them. This "feeling of oneself into" a contemplated object and the tendency to emotionally identify oneself with the object is what constitutes empathy.

The concept of empathy is of real use in understanding and criticizing pictures. It is particularly helpful in discovering the obscurer faults in pictures. To all appearances everything is correct and well arranged in a given composition: yet the picture is felt to be all wrong. Analysis may reveal *faulty empathy*. Perhaps, for example, the *thrust* of a certain line may not be sufficiently balanced by the *weight* of an opposing mass.

We are particularly sensitive to faults of empathy in nude pictures. We are quick to identify ourselves with any strain or discomfort that is depicted or implied. A sensitive and imaginative person may feel actual physical discomfort in contemplating a nude of faulty empathy.

Outrageous and distressing instances of faulty empathy in nudes can be found in the pages of any photographic journal or annual today.

A Black-List of Nudes.

It is a melancholy fact that the bad nudes in photographic journals, annuals and portfolios far exceed in number the good nudes. The bad nudes, indeed, are so predominant and common that one may observe a certain grotesque standardization in their badness. Numerous well-defined and readily recognizable types may be identified among them. It will prove useful to name and discuss some of these types, for nothing could give us a clearer impression of the importance of empathic considerations in nude photography.

A considerable number of these types owe their badness to various faults of empathy. Others are simply hackneyed, banal, or foolish. We will list the types of bad empathy first. For examples, simply thumb through any photographic publication.

First on the list is the previously discussed *Nujol nude*. This practice of drenching the body in oil creates a very unpleasant empathic impression of sliminess and uncleanliness. It also offends against the structure of the body by placing violent highlights in places where highlights have no business to be. A derivative of the Nujol nude is the *radiator-cap nude*. (Figure 180.)

The *mal de mer nude* bows her head in an affected posture. The negative, depressed attitude suggests either a great sorrow or impending nausea.

There is one type of nude that always gives the beholder a start of embarrassment and a desire to back out with confused apologies. This is the *prudy-nudy*. She disposes of her hands with such accuracy and cowers in such an ecstasy of modesty that the blushing observer feels a kindred embarrassment. The arch-priestess of the prudy-nudy cult is *September Morn*.

Occasionally one encounters a nude in which the curious and violent angles of the limbs suggest that an unpleasant accident has taken place. This we may designate as the *dislocated nude*. The faulty empathy is obvious.

218

Akin to the dislocated nude, and somewhat commoner, is the *pretzel nude*. In this
case the limbs are woven in circular and inter-
locking patterns. The bad empathy of this
contortionist feat is due to the sense of strain
and the denial of the normal structural relationships of the limbs.

We have already discussed and shown in
Part One an example of the *speckled nude*.
These cast shadows of Venetian blinds, foliage,
window-screens, etc., are all examples of bad
empathy. The imposed pattern of the shadows
is quite irrelevant to bodily structure, and the
suggestion of a mechanical pattern on the skin
is most unpleasant.

Examples of the *blubber nude* are all too
common in modern European photography.
These figures are embellished with rubber
tires around the middle and break out everywhere into lolloping rolls of flesh.

The blubber nude and certain related
species (the *pimpled nude* and the *hirsute
nude*) have constituted the so-called photographic purists' contribution to the art of the
nude—posterior views of fat women, massive
lumps of flesh, areas of unwholesome skin,
all rendered with the most meticulous atten-

tion to detail and texture.

It is undeniably true that there is a peculiar photographic pleasure to be obtained from the rendition of delicate detail, and that there is a world of new and unsuspected beauty to be found in the study of the surface textures of the most commonplace objects. But this passion for texture and detail is grotesquely inappropriate to the representation of the nude. The purists reason in the same fallacious vein as Katisha, the elderly and scantly appreciated Gilbert and Sullivan heroine. "I have a left shoulder blade that is a miracle of loveliness. People come miles to see it. My right elbow has a fascination that few can resist. It is on view Tuesdays and Fridays, on presentation of visiting card. As for my circulation, it is the largest in the world."

But the power and attraction of the nude does not reside in these *details*. Not the shoulder blade, not the elbow, not even the stupendous circulation, but the general plastic impression, is the thing of ultimate importance in a nude.

Another faulty type of nude, to return to our list, may be described as the *abraded nude*. The model is represented as sitting, reclining or lurking in surroundings that are utterly at variance with the delicacy of her nude body. The empathic reaction from the spectacle of a nude body seated on rough stone is exceedingly unpleasant, yet the act is often represented. Sometimes the model is represented as lying among harsh spikes of grass: more bad empathy.

Sometimes we see the model, white and pale of skin, posing in desert surroundings under a blazing Southern sun. This furnishes us with the *sun-burnt nude*.

An opposite type, but of equally bad empathy, is the *gooseflesh nude*. This unhappy model poses among the reeds at the pond's edge while the water laps coldly at her knees.

The foregoing nudes are all distinguished by bad empathy. There remains another group of equally characteristic and well-typed bad nudes that is marked not so much by faulty empathy as by banality. They represent the effort of the empty mind to create something "artistic" by falling back on stereotyped and vacuous formulas. They all pertain to the hollow and pretentious domain of fake art. Some of the poses that we are about to discuss have become a little too hackneyed for use on calendars, but they still occupy large space in the salons.

The first of these is the *hippity-hop nude* who prances her way with exhausting exuberance through the pages of foreign photographic annuals. Her arms are always upward-flung, she generally poses precariously on one toe, but her abandon occasionally leads her to leap into the air.

A sedate variant of this type is the *seaside-sunset-silhouette nude*. The elements are fairly constant: one setting sun, one breaking wave, one yard of crepe de chine, one piece of seaweed, and one lightly tripping nude who is outlined against the sky and the shining sand. Sometimes she appears in a more meditative and *mal de mer* attitude, and sometimes the scene is enlivened by the presence of *three* lightly tripping nudes and *three* yards of crepe de chine.

The useful fabric mentioned above has created its own type of nude. The *crepe de chine nude* takes us back to the happy innocent days of the first photographic nudes—days which must have been marked by peak production in the Brooklyn silk mills. Young men sallied forth on Sunday afternoons with their view cameras, their girl friends, and the necessary yard of fabric. A delicate and complicated technique was evolved for manipulating this fragile textile—floating it on the breeze in loops, volutes and swirls.

Related to both the crepe de chine nude and the prudy-nudy is the *portiere nude*. It is related to the latter by its slight touch of pudicity. The head is always turned modestly aside, and the two yards of velvet fall in discreet apron fashion down the front.

The *Tiffany nude* is decked with jewelry. Sometimes she approvingly regards the effect in a hand mirror, and sometimes she is just passively festooned with ropes of pearls, like a Christmas tree.

There is one type which suggests that the model has made herself very much at home in a gifte shoppe. This we may call the *knick-knack nude*. In this type there are generally present a couple of urns or vawses, a bearskin rug, a scarf draped with conscientious elegance, a crystal ball and a peacock fan.

The *Emily Post nude* is a very superior creature. She makes clear by her lofty and disdainful expression that she is above all this, knows instantly which fork to use, and understands perfectly the intricate problems of social precedence involved in introducing an archbishop to a grand duchess (or vice versa).

The final type is a very familiar one, the *Ah Me Nude* (sometimes known as the *Weltschmerz nude*). The pain of it all, the unsupportable cosmic pang, is the evident motive for her epic gesture of despair.

These are some of the nudes that we might just as well do without. The photographic world would be much better off if all Nujol nudes, *mal de mer* nudes, hippity-hop nudes, pretzel nudes, knick-knack nudes, etc., etc.,

etc., were to "suddenly and softly vanish away". I can hear protests that the elimination of these types of nudes would practically strip bare the pages of the photographic journals and the walls of the salons. To this horrendous prospect I would say, "Bravo!" Or I might even speak English and say, "Swell!"

For this cataclysm would still leave us well provided for. The masters of the past have left us an ample heritage of nudes done without benefit of Nujol, knickknacks or crepe de chine. And modern artists in black and white such as Norman Lindsay are still interpreting anew the wonder, dignity and divinity of the human body.

Figure and Personality.

The quest for the perfect figure is often a difficult and disappointing one. Models that have seemed to promise much when viewed with their clothes on will many times prove to be photographically hopeless when their clothes are removed. Because of the delicacy of the issues involved in the relationship of artist and model, it is most advisable that the artist learn to judge the excellence of the figure in advance without subjecting himself to the disappointment, or the model to the embarrassment, of an unsuccessful sitting in the nude.

It is helpful to realize that there is a frequent close relationship between personality and figure. Indeed, according to the opinion of a certain school of physiologists, physical lineaments and personality are derived from a common source—the functioning of the endocrine glands. Even if one does not accept their materialistic conclusions unreservedly, these physiologists are able to offer helpful suggestions to the puzzled artist.

There is, for example, a certain personality that is always proving a source of disappointment to the questing photographer of the nude. This is the woman of the clinging-vine type (the "post-pituitary" type, in the cant of the gland specialists). This sort is very deceptive, for she frequently has a Dresden china delicacy of features, with finely turned hands, wrists, feet and legs. But in the nude she proves to be lumpy of body, with wide hips and heavy breasts. An extremely tapered hand, beautiful but ineffectual, is a token of this type, and usually indicates wide hips.

The phlegmatic type of woman seldom has a good figure. Nor has the retiring, introspective type. Women with secrets have the worst figures of all.

The best models for photography of the nude will generally be found among the so-called "thyroid" types. These are characterized by energy and grace. Their faces are distinguished by a notable breadth of brow and by large and brilliant eyes. Their figures are slender and compact, with well-proportioned breasts, trim hips, and straight, finely shaped legs. Effective exaggerations of these characterists are furnished by the "hyper-thyroid" type.

The camera is notoriously prone to increase the apparent size and heaviness of the figure that it photographs. Therefore, for photographic purposes, a figure that is small and spare and tightly knit is to be preferred to one that inclines to voluptuousness or to Junoesque proportions. Figures of the noble sort that Michelangelo

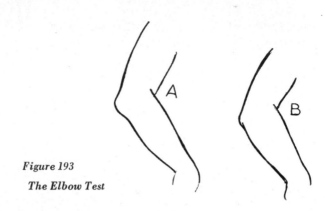

Figure 193

The Elbow Test

placed on the Sistine ceiling the camera would render as gross and overweight.

Realize also that the face is a very poor guide to the excellence of the figure. For some reason the Creator has very oddly assorted faces and figures, assigning beautiful heads to squat torsos, and crowning perfect bodies with very imperfect faces. My own observations indicate, for example, that a fine figure is quite apt to be accompanied with a receding chin.

The structure of the calves, ankles, elbows, neck and shoulders provide criterions by which the structure of the rest of the body may usually be safely judged. A calf diminishing into a *slender ankle*, although a conventional token of beauty, does not usually signify a good figure. On the contrary, such structure goes with a figure of the post-pituitary type, and indicates wide hips and thighs and heavy breasts. Rather, a fairly substantial foot and ankle without an unduly bulging calf should be sought for. Should it be desired, as a concession to popular standards, to thin the ankle somewhat, this may be easily accomplished on the negative or print.

If, when the joint is bent at right angles, the elbow bone protrudes noticeably (Figure 193, a), it is probable that the crest of the ilium (the hip bone) protrudes in a similar manner. In nudes, such a fault of the ilium is a serious blemish, as it breaks the smooth sweep of the contour line. Such a picture as *Youth*, for example, would be impossible to conceive or carry out if the line were interrupted by any irregularity at the hip.

Fashions and Figures.

Another influence on the female figure almost as potent as the glands is furnished by the commercial artist who draws the illustrations in the fashion journals. No more striking confirmation could be provided for Oscar Wilde's paradox that "Nature imitates Art". As the sunsets took on new colorations after Turner painted them, so the female figure hastened to assume the configuration that Erte ascribed to it. Certainly the "flapper"—who is not yet quite forgotten —was largely the result of Nature's imitation of John Held, Jr.'s, fantastic drawings.

Present day women's fashions are constructed for figures of the "adrenal" type—nervous, tightly-drawn, and masculine. This type of figure, and its jittery implications, is very unfortunate photographically. This is shown in the current photographic vogue of fashion magazines—angles, harsh, insistent and masculine; broken wrists; weird fore-shortenings; hyper-extended elbows; butchery by light. No trace of feminine grace is allowed to intrude; for it would slow down the violence of the action.

It seems to be a grave problem which will hold out the longer— Nature or the photographers. Many of their recent pictures suggest that with just one more twist the models will have to go to the hospital with broken bones, wrenched tendons, dislocated clavicles, and Charlie-horses.

Nudes Are Not All.

It has been necessary in this book to stress the structural basis of posing. For this reason there has been an emphasis on the nude. Do not be misled by this emphasis. Nudes are not the end all and be all of pictorial art. Nor are they the ultimate test of a model's usefulness. Nudes represent, after all, but a small fraction of the finest pictures. Many of the best pictorialists have never exhibited any nudes.

Nudes are a very difficult matter—both from the directorial and the pictorial point of view. Only the best of material and the finest of figures should be used. The taking of nude pictures should not be gone about in a hurry. Don't rush matters; let the question of posing in the nude be arrived at logically and naturally, when both artist and model are prepared for it.

The impetuous photographer who rushes into a sitting, flaunting the uncompromising motto of "Nudes or Nothing", inevitably comes to grief. At most he obtains a few snapshots of an alarmed, embarrassed and awkward girl without any clothes on. But no nudes. And the chances are about twenty to one that *that* model will never pose for him again.

Several sittings and numerous experiments with costume and costume elements should, as a rule, precede any work with the nude. And when you have finished, the probability is great that you will find that you have secured your best pictures in the earlier sittings.

The Use of Groups.

Many interesting pictorial projects require the use of several models. Group pictures of necessity come in the *plastic* category—with the artist dominant. Models that are normally of the cooperative type may be advantageously employed in group pictures, but they must subordinate themselves in the passive attitude of the plastic model. Unity in a group picture may be obtained only by the external influence of the artist in effecting coordination of the parts.

Group pictures require *careful preparation in advance.* Unless the sitting is to be a total loss, certain requisites must be well under control before getting under way. Among these pre-established requisites we may mention:

1. Generalized subject.
2. Several tentative sketches.
3. Correct number of models, chosen for type.
4. Costumes or costume elements suitable to subject.

5. Setting or selected location, with large properties in place.

6. Detailed accessories—hand properties, make up materials, pins, combs, scissors, brushes, cold cream, make up rags, and first-aid kit. All these in charge of some responsible individual.

Building the Group Picture.

Only when the requisites are present and under control should the building of the picture be undertaken.

As a rule, a single character will dominate the composition in a group picture. In constructing the picture, it will be built toward this *dominating character.*

Therefore, first establish the general position and the outline of the pose of the model who plays this dominating character. There is at this time no effort at detail or at refining the pose. With the principal figure maintaining, in a relaxed and easy manner, the general import of the pose, the model who plays the character of secondary importance is placed in position and his pose adjusted in relationship to the first one. There is still no effort at refining detail. Then the third model is placed and posed in relation to the other two. The other models (if any) are now added to the well organized group of three.

When the preliminary physical set-up is complete, the model in the dominating position is instructed to add the *emotional element* to his pose. His pose is now carefully adjusted for detail and errors are eliminated.

Finally, all the other models in the group take the emotionalized version of their pose, and are subjected to adjustment and elimination of errors.

In this stage of final adjustment it will be found advantageous to get fresh angles and aspects of the picture in formation—to take the picture by surprise, as it were. Various expedients are resorted to in order to get this freshened vision: looking away from the picture for a moment and then looking back suddenly; looking at

"*A Family Group—Xmas 1914*"   *William Mortensen*

the picture with the head turned sideways; looking at it upside-down between the legs. Under this sort of scrutiny new relationships will discover themselves, incipient notan patterns and linear rhythms* will ask to be emphasized, and egregious errors will suddenly become evident. In this manner one is able to surprise a glimpse of the picture as a whole instead of the collection of details that one has been laboring with.

In the final stages of adjustment start taking exposures. Take

---

*Further treatment of these matters must await the completion of the author's volume on Composition.

many exposures. Much effort is expended in assembling the numerous elements that go into a group picture. Usually considerable expense is involved in bringing them together. It is the worst kind of economy under these circumstances to be stingy of exposures. Every time a slight adjustment is made in the set-up, record it with a new set of exposures.

The first idea of the picture, as planned and sketched, should not be regarded as a canon to be adhered to, but simply as a point of departure. In working with a group, variants from the original set-up will invariably suggest themselves. Often the gesture or reaction of a subordinate character will suggest a fresh set-up with this character in the dominating position. These hints and suggestions should be acted upon, for they will frequently prove to be the genesis of pictures more expressive and spontaneous than the one originally planned.

Personal Relationships in Dealing with Groups.

Dealing with a group of models in such a manner as to secure the best possible physical and emotional response is a problem of considerable complexity. The following suggestions will prove useful in keeping the sitting running smoothly.

To avoid interruptions annoying and distracting to the models the photographer should keep track carefully of the mechanical complications of his camera and lights. For models to be worked up to a difficult pose and violent emotional state and then be forced to wait indefinitely while film is changed or lights are juggled is an unjustifiable hardship as well as an anti-climax.

The sitting is put on a much more familiar and cooperative basis if the photographer will take pains to learn and *use* the *first names* of all the models. For some reason, a model responds far more readily and wholeheartedly when addressed as John or Mary than as Mr. Smith or Miss Jones.

Be careful, in giving directions to models, always to prefix the direction with the model's name. To give the name after the direction is almost as bad as giving no name at all. Much time and energy is lost in group sittings through failure to observe this simple rule. If the photographer says, for example, "Turn your head to the right, John", every head in the group will either turn, or start to turn, as directed. Each person of the group is on the *qui vive* for direction, and will be unconsciously resentful to discover he has been misled. On the other hand, "John, turn your head to the right", secures instant and efficient response where it is desired.

In a group of models there are bound to be rivalries and incipient jealousies. The one in the subordinate position is very sure that he (or she) is just as good as the one in the featured spot. The Second Grave Digger is certain to feel that he is uniquely qualified for the role of Hamlet. To keep peace in the family, and to prevent these jealousies from taking root, the photographer will be wise to see that in the course of his changes in set-up, every one of his models gets a chance at a featured position. This does not necessarily mean switching the roles about; for it is conceivable that an interesting picture and a fresh conception of the situation might result from subordinating Hamlet to the Second Grave Digger.

CHAPTER FOUR

The Personality Model.

The second condition of working with the model is that in which the model is dominant. The model in this case is designated as the "personality type".

A wide variety of subjects is embraced under this term. It includes professional persons, stage and screen actresses, authors, public figures. statesmen, and all such celebrities. It includes children, babies, dogs and cats. It includes persons, perhaps otherwise unknown to fame, who are notable for being "types" or "characters", or for possessing unusual facial quirks. It includes, finally, all sitters for "commercial portraits".

In all these cases the model is the dominant factor in the sitting. The photographer is the passive means of recording the fact that is set before him. His artistic task consists in giving this fact the most effective presentation.

To discuss adequately the multitudinous problems of so-called "commercial portraiture" would lead us far beyond the scope of this book. As typical problems involving the use of "personality models", I will consider only three of the subjects mentioned in the list above: the celebrity, the child as a pictorial model, and the building of a picture around a personal "quirk".

Photographing the Celebrity.

To nearly every photographer comes at some time opportunity to photograph a celebrity. The celebrity may be a minor one—but,

"Nils Asther"   *William Mortensen*

nevertheless, a Personage. It is very much to the advantage of the photographer to be able to make the most of such an opportunity; for there is an undeniable professional prestige to be gained through association with the great or near-great. To have made one effective portrait of George Bernard Shaw, for example, would bring one more kudos than a thousand excellent portraits of nonentities.

When such an opportunity presents itself, the photographer must first of all realize that he is to deal with a model of the dominant "personality" type. In other words, the photographer's role is not to be that of the Great Creative Artist; but simply that of the alert and efficient recording instrument.

If he is not already informed, the photographer should be careful to find out all he can about his celebrity in advance of the sitting. This research is useful in two ways. In the first place it gives a clue to the appropriate sort of pictorial treatment, which would naturally vary according to whether the celebrity was a pugilist, a philosopher, a trapeze artist or a singer. Secondly, the fact that the photographer is well-informed about him is gratifying to the inevitable and natural vanity of his subject.

If he has the opportunity, the photographer should look at other and former pictures of his prospective subject; for the celebrity is apt to be conservative in his tastes and to wish to be presented more or less as he has been presented.

The photographer must not be shocked to find, when he meets the Personage, that the latter holds photographers in general in very low esteem, and is apt to state that none of them have been able to capture the elusive quality of his personality.

In his conference with his subject before the sitting, he will of course take pains to find out the latter's wishes. He will be told one of two things:

    1. "I want my picture to be thus and thus and thus."

    2. "I leave it to you."

In the former case, he will try to fulfill the instructions as fully as possible. In the latter case, he will realize that this attitude, while allowing him a little more freedom, by no means gives him carte

William Mortensen

blanche in the sitting, for the subject's personality is still the principal issue.

Roughly speaking there are two general types of celebrities. One is the sort whose face and personality is their stock in trade. This is the "Personal Appearance" type of celebrity. To this class belong, of course, the well-known personalities of stage and screen. Here also must be grouped some of our statesmen. Mae West may be regarded as the archetype of this class.

Celebrities of this type are greatly dependent on public favor. They have a carefully evolved pseudo-personality which represents them before the public. This fictitious, synthetic personality must, of course, be the only phase of them that is presented in a picture. To portray Mae West, for example, digging in her garden, dressed in slacks and her hair falling in her eyes, would be quite disastrous to the public-personality which she has created and carefully fostered. Of course, this canny lady would never assent to such portrayal, and it would be a foolhardy photographer that would attempt it.

Whether or not this synthetic personality has any substance of truth in it, whether it represents at all the real person, is a completely alien issue. The photographer of the celebrity must make up his mind that it is not his business to be a crusader for truth or an iconoclastic revealer of sham. His job is simply to carry on the tradition that the celebrity represents.

The second type of celebrity is the sort whose contact with the public is not direct, through his face and personality, but indirect, through his work. To this class belong authors, scientists, artists and musicians.

A splendid example of photography of this type of celebrity is afforded by Steichen's dignified portrait of H. G. Wells.*

Although celebrities of this sort are, as a rule, much less dictatorial about the treatment of their pictures, the fact does not give any greater freedom to the artist. Personality is still the domi-

*See Camera Craft. January, 1936.

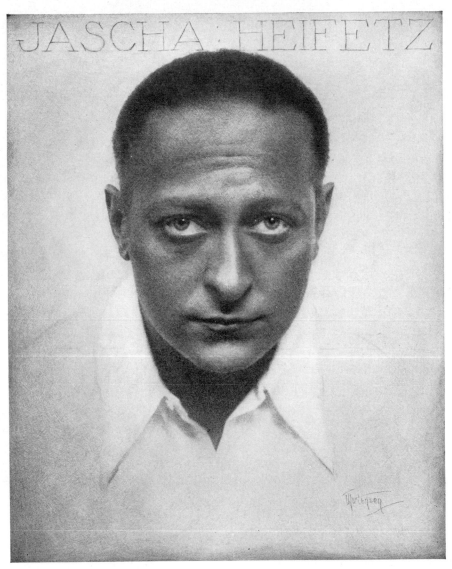

William Mortensen

nant issue, although in this case there is seldom any problem of maintaining a synthetically created personality. Equally with the first type there must be a complete absence of obvious influence by the artist. This is what is so finely realized in Steichen's portrait: it is H. G. Wells as H. G. Wells, *not* H. G. Wells as the Great Author.

The photographer must be prepared to find, when he looks over his proofs, that he has gotten some bad angles of his sitter's head. Indeed, some of the proofs are apt to suggest that the Great Man is not quite so wise, noble or honest as he is reputed. The photographer should not be discouraged or alarmed at finding these grotesque lapses from greatness among his proofs. He must realize that all the standard likenesses of the celebrity have undoubtedly been carefully selected. All these bad proofs should be destroyed. It is an excellent gesture of good faith to destroy both the bad proofs and the corresponding negatives in the presence of the subject.

Now, it is not likely that many of you who read this will have an opportunity to photograph either Mae West or H. G. Wells, but it is entirely within reason that you may wish to photograph the politically ambitious state senator or the author of pulp magazine "westerns" who is stopping in your town. The same general truths hold, and the same procedure should be followed. The state senator would, presumably, belong to the Mae West category, and would demand to be presented with the same consideration for *his* carefully synthesized personality of statecraft, sagacity, and love for the common people. The western author would fall in the Wells class, and would require to be shown objectively and without elaboration, "as is".

The Child as a Model.

Is is traditional on the stage that children and dogs always "steal the show". This is because both children and dogs are always uncompromisingly *themselves* and stand out in shocking three-dimensional contrast to the flat, conventionalized theatrical figures of the other actors.

Occasionally a child will be found that makes a very fine model.

"Doris"   *William Mortensen*

Its pictures will have a strangely arresting quality that may surprise even the photographer himself. This element which a child contributes to a picture is its *own*, and is not the result of direction or interpretation.

Although an intelligent child may take some direction, it still remains primarily a "personality model". Little preparation is possible in working with a child model, except in technical and material matters. Much dependence must be placed on waiting for the expressive moment and happy accident.

Discretion must be exercised in the choice of pictorial themes for the child model. It is ill fitted to the interpretive or emotional roles, but its strong personal appeal makes it very effective for a bit of sentiment.

The Personal Quirk.

Every day we meet and see people that are characterized by odd and individual tricks of expression—a knowing lift of the eyebrow, a one-sided smile, or a quaintly vagrant lock of hair. These quirks are frequently very effective pictorially. In securing these quirk portraits we have to do with another problem of the "personality model".

In a sitting with such a model the artist must be very much on the alert to catch the desired expression "on the fly", so to speak. Quick shooting is often necessary to do this. This kind of portrait, however, has nothing to do with the candid camera, or any of its works. Something depends on the happy accident of getting such a portrait, but it is an accident that is planned and schemed for. Preliminary analysis prepares one to take advantage of the accident when and if it happens.

At the sitting such a model is very apt to put on a conventional and "party" air that effectively smothers the desired quirk. Considerable skill is frequently demanded to call it forth again. This was the case with *Wong* (Figure 194). Wong was a Chinese cook and had been for many years a familiar figure around town as he went about his shopping with a huge market basket on his arm. I had

"*Wong*"   *William Mortensen*

Figure 194

noted the wise and humorous twinkle in his eye, and had long wanted to take a picture of him as I saw him every day. He was very pleased when I asked him to pose for me. To my consternation, he arrived for his sitting, not in his everyday cook's garb, but in his stiff and conventional Sunday best, with pince nez astride his nose, his hair slicked back, and his face as devoid of expression as his starched collar. Of course, it was necessary first to take the pictures that he wanted. Then, only by extended diplomacy and super-oriental wiles was I able to cover up the black coat, coax away the glasses, release his hair to follow its natural bent, and, finally, to lure back his own characteristic expression.

CHAPTER FIVE

The Cooperative Model

The cooperative model may be defined as standing between, and sometimes a little above, the plastic model and the personality model. It stands between them because it combines the phases of the artist-dominant situation and the model-dominant situation that respectively characterize these two. It stands above them because the finest pictures are based on such cooperation between artist and model.

The degree and kind of cooperation that the model gives will vary widely in individual cases. Both the plastic model and the personality model (especially of the "quirk" type) may, through intelligence and experience before the camera, work into the "cooperative" way of doing things. Since they approach the cooperative condition from opposite sides—one from an artist-dominant situation and the other from a model-dominant situation—it follows that the quality of their cooperation is quite different. We may thus distinguish two types of cooperation.

1. The first type consists in an *intelligent* reaction to plastic procedure and conditions. The pure plastic model is merely passively receptive. Examples of this plastic-cooperative condition are afforded by *The Tantric Sorcerer* (*Pictorial Lighting*, pg. 65) and *Market Girl* (*Monsters & Madonnas*).

2. In the second type of cooperation, the model simply acts out

the scene or character which he has himself conceived and prepared —and, in some cases, costumed. The artist observes and catches the *pictorial* aspects of what the model does. This way of working lends itself to scenes and characters depending upon subtleties of facial expression. These subtleties, of course, do not permit of plastic adjustment. *Napoleon* as posed by Peter Lorre (Figure 195) is an illustration of the personality-cooperative condition of working.

Few models are able to enter into full and complete cooperation with the artist. Although this condition may be productive of fine pictures, it is dangerously unstable and may readily degenerate into an impossible situation leading to boredom, antagonism, and mutual contempt. The artist must, therefore, exercise much discretion in admitting models to this footing of complete cooperation.

Ways of Cooperation.

There are numerous ways in which a model may usefully co-operate with the artist.

The simplest sort of cooperation is that which a plastic or personality type of model is able to give as soon as he or she has had a little experience before the camera—quick and ready response to directorial commands. With increasing experience the model is able to give more *intelligent* cooperation: he or she begins to appreciate the two-dimensional limitations of the pictorial medium, and acquires some knowledge of plastic faults or errors that are to be avoided.

An interested and enthusiastic model is often able to give much assistance in assembling costumes or building sets.

An intelligent model is frequently valuable in working out research problems. Research is a very important phase of picture making. Its importance lies not so much in the elements of literal fact and physical accuracy that it contributes, but in the added richness of background and understanding that one is enabled to bring to bear upon the problem.

The model may also cooperate by suggesting pictorial ideas and in conferring with the artist preliminary to the sitting. Here we touch on debatable ground. Excellent pictorial suggestions are

"Napoleon, Portrayed by Peter Lorre"　　　　　　　　　　　*William Mortensen*

Figure 195

sometimes offered by models, but the artist must be exceedingly chary in accepting them.

The Pattern and Procedure of a Sitting.

There is a great deal more to taking a picture than merely setting up the camera and the model opposite each other, taking a few exposures and calling it a day. A sitting is a psychological problem of hidden mental and spiritual forces even more than it is a physical problem of tangible elements such as cameras, lighting units, films, etc., etc. *A sitting is a creative act,* and as such it should conform to the universal dramatic pattern of such acts.

Let me outline this pattern.

1. Begin the sitting with a definite and positive act. It is dangerous, not to say fatal, to start on a note of doubt, of hesitation, of "Let me see, now—". Assurance is needed throughout the sitting, but especially at the beginning. The artist's motto should be "Leap before you look". So—begin the sitting with an act. It is not crucially important what this act is. If you can think of nothing better, move your front lighting unit, with a firm and determined gesture, two inches to the right. Or tell the model to sit up straighter. Or say to your model, "Excellent!"—and immediately take an exposure.

2. By this initial act—whatever it was—you have created *something tangible.* You now have a point to carry on from. One act suggests another act. Keep on going along the line you have started. Vacillation now weakens the whole structure and largely vitiates the advantage you have secured by your initial act.

3. Suggestions will now begin to spontaneously assert themselves. Acting on these suggestions, make a few simple modifications of your basic idea. At this point you will have succeeded in recording the prosaic, rational substance of the model's pose.

4. Now that you are in control of the situation, the cooperative aspect of the model may assert itself. It is very dangerous at any earlier stage in the sitting to ask for or accept any suggestions from the model. By now the model's interest will be aroused. The sitting is beginning to move; you are getting somewhere. The model's in-

terest shows itself by *participation*, instead of mere acquiescence, in the sitting, and by quick instinctive anticipation of your wishes. The model may at this point offer suggestions. These may be acted upon, because they come from one who, equally with you, is carried along on the mental current you have created.

5. The current now becomes a torrent and sweeps you irresistibly with it. At the height of this experience there occurs a strange feeling of *clarity*. All things seem simple and easy. You may at this stage in the sitting try the craziest of things and bring them off triumphantly; for you will be sustained by the force you have evoked.

6. Although toward the end of the sitting you are exhausted in mind and body, the model may still be seething with interest and fresh ideas. This interest should be satisfied, for good results are often secured in this final stage of the sitting.

Where Shall I Find Models?

Every once in a while I receive a piteous appeal from some photographic amateur who has, it seems, everything his heart desires except something to take pictures of. One writes to this effect: "I live in a small town, and there are no models available. What shall I do?" Another states: "I live in a large city, and I don't know where to look for models. What shall I do?"

There is no secret in finding models, no need for extensive search, no necessity to know "the right people". Just look about you. Unless you are a hermit, there is probably a very good model within fifty feet of you at this moment.

To find models it is merely necessary to keep your eyes open and cultivate a critical appreciation of physical structure. The waitress who brought your coffee and doughnuts this morning may be a potential Sistine Madonna, and the brat who sold you a paper may be a Fra Angelico cherub. Among your friends, neighbors and relatives there are undoubtedly models of unsuspected ability.

The painters of the past were never stopped for any lack of models. They haled in porters and fishwives from the streets and children from the gutters and made saints and angels of them. They made keen and critical likenesses of their fellow burghers and their wives. And, just to keep their hand in, they looked in the mirror and made self-portraits.

"But what shall I do," I am asked, "when I see a bootblack, newsboy or waitress that I would like to have pose for me?" The answer is simple: Ask them. In asking them you are participating in a gamble in which the cards are stacked in your favor. The chances are at least nine in ten that the person will accept. Everyone is susceptible to flattery. The implication, or perhaps outright statement, that the person is "just the type" that you have been seeking is flattery of the most effective sort.

The art schools in the larger cities are able to supply the inquirer with information and references to models. There are also models' bureaus or agencies. The professional models that one obtains through these channels are, however, very limited in their usefulness. Except for pictures along strictly conventional lines, such as fashion plates, they are rarely satisfactory. Modelling is for them merely a business, and they go through their ritual with disinterested, mechanical precision.

The good pictures that I have secured from professional models have been very few indeed. My best results have been obtained from non-professionals—people who have had little or no previous experience before the camera. Some of them have been friends of mine, some of them have been casual acquaintances, and some of them (up to the moment that I asked them to pose) have been perfect strangers. From models such as these one obtains the utmost of interest, enthusiasm, vitality and cooperation.

Learn to see the pictorial qualities of the people that you meet and pass by every day. Don't let your quest for a particular type of model render you unaware of the capacities of others. In your obsessing search for a perfect feminine figure, for example, you may be ignoring the pictorial possibilities of the patriarchal shoemaker on the corner and of the quaint dressmaker up the side street.

Anything human that can be coaxed in front of a camera is potentially a model. That which is in front of the camera is the indispensable basis of photographic art. The model, however, furnishes merely the basis. The word of command, the creative act that calls forth the pictorial form from this unformed flesh, can proceed only from the artist. . . . The model awaits you, the camera is ready, the lights are set. The rest is up to you.

APPENDIXES

APPENDIX A

The Rights of the Model.

Releases.

The photographer may not exhibit, sell or publish a picture without having secured the permission of the model who has posed for it. It is therefore advisable that the photographer always protect himself by securing a written release of the model's rights in the picture. Failure to take this precaution may land the photographer in a great deal of unpleasantness and possible legal difficulty, particularly if nude pictures are involved.

The following form is suggested for such releases:

RELEASE FORM FOR ADULTS

...., 193......

In consideration of............................'s taking photographs of me, I hereby irrevocably authorize him, in his discretion, for his own account and without control of any kind by me (and whether such photographs be taken now or at any time in the future), to use, display, sell, publish, modify, alter, combine with others, and otherwise treat or deal with any or all such photographs and any and all plates, films, prints, copies, enlargements, etchings, modifications, alterations, combinations and other treatments thereof, hereby conveying to him all property rights and privileges in connection therewith as well as in connection with any photographs heretofore taken by him, together with the right to confer any or all such rights and privileges upon others, without obligation of any kind by him or anyone else except that my services for modelling shall be paid for at the rate

of .... per hour.

(Signed)..

Witness:..

If the model is a minor, the release must be signed by parent or guardian. The following form may be used in this case:

RELEASE FORM FOR MINORS

...., 193.........

In consideration of...'s taking photographs of my daughter (son) ....,
I hereby irrevocably authorize him, in his discretion, for his
own account and without control of any kind by me (and
whether such photographs be taken now or at any time in the
future), to use, display, sell, publish, modify, alter, combine
with others, and otherwise treat or deal with any and all such
photographs and any and all such plates, films, prints, copies,
enlargements, etchings, modifications, alterations, combinations and other treatments thereof, hereby conveying to him
all property rights and privileges in connection therewith as
well as in connection with any photographs heretofore taken
by him, together with the right to confer any or all such
rights and privileges upon others, without obligation of any
kind by him or anyone else except that my daughter (son)
shall receive..per hour for her (his)
services as a model.

(Signed)...

Witness:...

In order to prevent misunderstanding and possible loss of time
and material, releases should always be arranged for and signed
before the final prints are made. If the model has not previously
posed in the nude, it is poor strategy to alarm her by bringing up
the release and its suggested legal complications before the sitting.
But when she is shown some excellent proofs and a fine test print,
she will generally prove quite amenable in the matter of signing the
release—particularly if the photographer makes it clear that he can

go no further in making pictures until the release is arranged for.

Compensation.

The labourer is worthy of his hire; and the model, if he or she merits the expenditure of time and material, is entitled to compensation.

The photographer should no more expect a model to pose for him without compensation than he would expect a dentist to fill his teeth without payment or a butcher to supply him with pork chops *gratis.* The amount and nature of the compensation should be definitely understood before starting the sitting. This understanding is an immediate aid toward placing the relationship on a businesslike and impersonal basis.

The payment may take the form of prints or cash. The latter, being less debatable in value, is the preferable form—if the artist can afford it. The amount of payment may be somewhat adjusted to meet the model's ability and the artist's capacity to pay. I suggest a dollar an hour as a moderate and reasonable fee for the model— with a minimum of a dollar if the sitting runs for less than an hour.

If the photographer is inclined to demur at this price, let him remember that in an hour's time he would probably use a great deal more than a dollar's worth of film. The model is entitled to at least as much credit as Eastman, Gevaert or Agfa.

This scale of compensation is suggested as appropriate for the pictorial worker, who seldom realizes any substantial monetary return from his pictures. However, the commercial photographer in the advertising field can properly afford larger payment. Indeed, some of the best commercial models in New York command fees upward of twenty-five dollars an hour.

Regarding the Sale of Pictures.

The signing of a release by the model affords legal protection for the photographer. But he must not feel that he is thereby released from moral obligations.

A photographer who becomes known for his work with the nude will in the natural course of events receive numerous offers to purchase prints—some for advertising purposes, and some for private delectation.

The sale of nude pictures to private individuals is risky business —even with releases duly signed and witnessed—and does not add to the reputation of any photographer. The best way to meet such offers is to quote prices sufficiently large to discourage further negotiation.

The advisability of the sale of pictures—nude or otherwise— for advertising purposes depends entirely upon the kind of advertising. Before selling, the photographer should be assured of the dignity and worth of the use to which his picture—and his model— are to be put.

The signed release is the model's expression of confidence that the picture will not be put to an unworthy use. The photographer's prospect for success depends in large measure upon the good will of his models. This good will may be maintained only by keeping up his reputation for consideration and fair dealing.

Inquiries.

The photographer must exercise the greatest of discretion in giving out information regarding his models.

When pictures are published or exhibited, curiosity is always aroused in some quarters regarding the identity of the persons posing for them. The photographer should be prepared to receive—and politely to divert—many inquiries on this subject.

A *few* of these inquiries may merit consideration—i.e., questions from *bona fide* theatrical agents or producers. A photographer must be very certain that it is to the possible advantage of his model to be put in touch with an inquirer. And he should *never, under any circumstances,* send the address or name directly to the correspondent. The letter should be turned over to the model, and the final responsibility left with her.

The majority of inquiries are not legitimate, and seem to imply that the photographer is a sort of pictorial Pandarus always willing to oblige with specifications and telephone numbers.

The following formula is suggested as a tactful method of discouraging such inquiries:

Dear Mr. Blotz:

It is some years since I photographed the lady you ask about, so I am unfortunately unable to provide you with her address.

However, I am happy to be able to inform you that for some time past her two eldest sons have been living in Chicago, where one of them has been working as brakeman for the New York Central.

His present address is 1224 Gilhooley Ave. Owing to the exigencies of his profession, he is seldom at home; but if you enquire there, one of the children will undoubtedly be able to inform you of their grandmother's whereabouts.

Hoping this information will prove useful to you, and that you will continue to favor me with your little problems,

Cordially yours,

APPENDIX B

Self-Protective Precautions.

In Appendix A I mentioned some of the rights, legal and moral, of the model. The model is entitled to protection from cheap exploitation and from unauthorized use of his or her picture.

The photographer likewise is liable to certain perils in his dealings with models, and the inexperienced worker may find himself in a serious predicament unless he takes proper precautions.

The first, most elementary and most important of these precautions is: *Be sure that releases are signed by all models.* The release protects the artist equally with the model and insures him against embarrassment and possible lawsuits. Careless photographers pay through the nose every year because their failure to observe this simple precaution gives the models a chance to tell the judge that their reputation has suffered a hurt that can only be soothed in a substantial monetary way.

If a photographer does much work with models, he should protect himself with some form of liability insurance. The hazard to life and limb that a model undergoes is not great, as a rule, but there is always the possibility of an accident serious enough to give a disgruntled or litigiously inclined model an excuse to bring suit. And there are remote but genuine risks that should be guarded against: a model may be injured by the collapse of a setting, or by tipping over heavy lighting equipment, or she may catch cold on a location trip and fall ill with pneumonia. All liability for such accidents may be taken care of by insurance.

There is another sort of risk that the artist should guard against: damage to his self-esteem. Occasionally one encounters a highly independent model who wants to hedge the photographer about with humiliating restrictions. She will say, for example, "Yes, I will pose for you. But I must inspect all your negatives and you must destroy all those that I do not approve of. Nor shall you make any prints from any negatives except by my permission." If the model is very lovely, the temptation may be strong to humbly knuckle under and meet all conditions in the remote hope of somehow salvaging a picture. A much wiser plan is to tell such a model to take her beautiful body and jump into the lake with it. For an artist to accept such restrictions is for him to surrender his directorial prerogative by giving the model the upper hand. This directorial prestige is all-important to him; without it he is just a candid cameraman. Nor should the photographer fail to note the insult implied in suggesting such restrictions: she says, in effect, "I do not consider you a good enough artist to make a selection from my negatives, nor do I consider you a sufficiently honest man to be trusted with them."

Finally, we come to a more insidious risk against which the photographer is best protected by simply being aware of its existence. It is a fact that the peculiar circumstances of nude photography provide an ideal setting for a frame-up. Amateur photographers are often persons of means and sufficiently concerned about their standing in their communities to constitute perfect victims for some variant of the old badger game. This risk is a genuine one: I know of several artists who have paid up rather than submit themselves to the notoriety of an unsavory lawsuit.

In view of this danger, it behooves a photographer to be very careful in his selection of models, and to inform himself, whenever possible, of their background and reputation. He may further protect himself, in the event that it is not feasible or advantageous for a third person to be present in the studio during the sitting, by making sure, when he is employing a new or unknown model, that he has a representative in an adjoining room. And he will, of course, avoid any episodes or circumstances in the sitting that might give confirmatory colour to subsequent allegations. For this reason, he will not have the sitting late at night, nor will he locate his studio in a remote or inaccessible spot. For this reason, also, he will carefully restrain any lush or Oriental tastes that he may have in matters of interior decoration. A studio should be obviously and frankly a work-room—not a replica of a high-class bordello.

APPENDIX C

Analysis of Faulty Nudes.

Following is the author's analysis of the faulty nudes shown in Figures 116, 117, 118 and 119 in Chapter Six:

Figure 116:

    Slumped scapula (Figure 83)
    Hyper-extended elbow (Figure 49)
    Collapsed wrist (Figure 66)
    Bottom of foot (Figure 113)
    Leathery elbow

Figure 117:

    Head thrown back too far (Figure 15)
    Elbow trap (Figure 46)
    Upper arm crushed against body (Figure 57)
    Collapsed wrist on supporting arm (Figure 66)
    Flattened fanetta (Figure 87)
    Knee stump (Figure 101)

Figure 118:

    Butchery by light
    Head thrown back too far (Figure 15)
    Wrist cut by drapery
    Spread fingers

Figure 119:

Broken wrists (Figure 65)
Arm from nowhere (Figure 53)
Knee stumps (Figure 101)
Hyper-extended elbow (Figure 49)
"Error of outlying parts" (Figure 121)

In addition to containing the listed plastic errors, Figures 117 and 118 are fairly typical examples of the "Ah Me" nude described in Chapter Three of Part Three.